PROBLEMS IN
LITERARY RESEARCH:

A Guide to Selected Reference Works

by

DOROTHEA KEHLER

with the assistance of
Fidelia Dickinson

The Scarecrow Press, Inc.

Metuchen, N.J.   1975

Library of Congress Cataloging in Publication Data

Kehler, Dorothea, 1936-
    Problems in literary research.

    Includes index.
    1. Reference books--Literature.   2.   Literary re-
search.   I.   Dickinson, Fidelia.   II.   Title.
Z6511. K4   [PN523]   808'. 02   75-16427
ISBN 0-8108-0841-2
ISBN 0-8108-0842-0 (Instructor's Index)

To the memory of my mother,

Minnie Coopersmith Gutwill

CONTENTS

PREFACE

Both a reference guide and a textbook, <u>Problems in Literary Research</u> is designed to introduce students of literature to some of the most useful library resources and to bring to the librarian's attention those resources most valuable to the literary researcher. The emphasis is upon English and American literature, but many entries have bearing on the study of comparative literature or particular foreign literatures.

Though no one would question the necessity for being acquainted with the library's basic reference holdings, nevertheless, students drawn to literature <u>con amore</u> are often dismayed by the extent and detail of the material they are expected to master--usually within a semester. I have sought to make the introduction to literary research less formidable by selecting works that are fundamental, either in themselves or as representatives of a class of reference tools. These works constitute the thirty-six main entries (the "M's"), which are sufficient to survey the field but not to boggle the mind. Contents and arrangement are outlined at some length in order to expedite the process of gaining familiarity with these works.

The Review Questions are primarily intended to reinforce absorption of the information provided in the outlines. Since many of these questions are intentionally hypothetical or general, the student should attempt to formulate his answers without consulting the reference work described. Hopefully, he will recognize most of the subjects suggested as examples of possible entries. Class discussion of the Review Questions can serve to identify unfamiliar examples. The Research Problems which follow can be solved through the exclusive use of the work just introduced. Each of the General Review problems can be solved by employing one of the works introduced up to that point; here, too, each problem requires the use of only a single reference work. However, in the case of a few dual entries (<u>Comprehensive Dissertation Index</u>

and <u>Dissertation Abstracts International</u>), a single problem may call for both works.

Under Supplementary Works (the "S" entries), I have briefly described alternative and additional reference tools. Those preceded by an asterisk are important to all literature students. As for the other supplementary works, the student should be aware of their existence so that he can consult those relevant to his particular needs. In the headnotes and footnotes I have supplied bibliographic data only for works not given "S" entries; the scope of these "non-S" works can generally be inferred from their full titles.

Like most reference guides, <u>Problems in Literary Research</u> is necessarily selective and sometimes arbitrary in its classifications. I have omitted some excellent alternative works only because they are not significantly different from the main or supplementary entries. Students will easily discover these alternatives by themselves because similar reference works are most often shelved beside each other. I have used my own judgment in classifying works that overlap two categories or that are best studied together with a companion tool (a variorum edition and a concordance).

Two <u>caveats</u> are appropriate here. First, the student should avail himself of the most recent edition of any reference work as well as its current supplements. When using these works in the course of his professional career, he should be alert to updatings. With a few notable exceptions (Britannica, perhaps <u>The Cambridge Bibliography of English Literature</u>), the most recent edition is the only one suitable for scholarly research. Second, insofar as reference tools are secondary, not primary sources, few of the works entered are suitable for quoting in scholarly papers. In doubtful cases, it is always wise to follow the practice of established scholars.

I have found several books especially useful in compiling this guide: Constance Winchell's <u>Guide To Reference Books</u>, Bohdan S. Wynar's <u>Introduction to Bibliography and Reference Work,</u> Rolland E. Stevens' <u>Reference Books in the Social Sciences and Humanities,</u> and Richard D. Altick and Andrew Wright's <u>Selective Bibliography for the Study of English and American Literature</u>. I am also indebted to Fidelia Dickinson, Associate Director of the San Diego State University Library, for her numerous valuable suggestions and research; to Phillip Smith, Reference Librarian at the University of California, San Diego, for his generous assistance;

to Cheryl Carroll, Elizabeth Gebur, Linda Gratteau and Eve Kehler for checking many of the research problems; to my husband for reading the manuscript; and above all to my students for their encouragement and appreciation.

D. K.

CHAPTER I

A BASIC CORE

M1. The Oxford Companion to English Literature

M2. The Oxford Companion to American Literature

M3. A Literary History of England

M4. Literary History of the United States: History

M5. The New Cambridge Bibliography of English Literature

M6. Literary History of the United States: Bibliography

M7. MLA International Bibliography

M8. The Oxford English Dictionary

The reference tools introduced in this chapter constitute a survival kit for the English major. They are the most basic of works: a handbook, a literary history, and a bibliography for English and American literature respectively; an international bibliography for updating bibliographies awaiting supplements or new editions; and a (one should say "the") historical dictionary. The value of these tools is so great that the student will surely want to purchase several of them for his personal library.

M1. The Oxford Companion to English Literature. Ed. Sir Paul Harvey. 4th ed., rev. Dorothy Eagle. Oxford: Clarendon Press, 1967.

The OCEL or "Harvey," a capsule-information handbook, belongs to the useful Oxford Companion Series, many

1

of whose titles have some bearing on the study of literature.
The OCEL is more comprehensive than its title suggests, insofar as it includes a fair number of non-English authors,
literary terms, etc.   Other Oxford Companion titles include
The Oxford Companion to American Literature (M2); The Oxford Companion to the Theatre (S18); The Oxford Companion
to French Literature (S27); The Oxford Companion to Classical Literature (S25); Norah Story, The Oxford Companion to
Canadian History and Literature (Toronto: Oxford University
Press, 1967, Supplement, 1973); Thomas H. Johnson, The Oxford Companion to American History (New York: Oxford University Press, 1966); Percy Alfred Scholes, The Oxford Companion to Music, 9th ed. corr. (London: Oxford University
Press, 1960); and The Oxford Companion to Art, ed. Harold
Osborne (Oxford: Clarendon Press, 1970).

Though a particular Companion may not be the ultimate
dictionary-guide in its field, nevertheless, these Oxford titles
are worth keeping in mind as reputable fact-finders for basic
literary and literature-related research.

Contents:

1)   Authors (mostly English but some significant American
     and European):[1] biographies and works with their
     dates.[2]
2)   Works: their nature; if a major work, a plot sum-
     mary.
3)   Characters (fictional and historical);   under surname
     unless an indissoluble whole (Peter Pan).
4)   Literary groups and movements.
5)   Allusions: proper names (includes non-literary and
     mythological figures associated with English literature;
     place names;[3] literary terms.[4]
6)   Appendices:
     a.   "Censorship and the Law of the Press":   an es-
          say on the censorship of literature, journalism,
          and theatrical performances from the sixteenth
          century through modern times.
     b.   "Notes on the History of the English Copyright."
     c.   "The Calendar":   an essay and tables on the Julian
          and Gregorian calendars, saints' days and church
          feasts, and regnal years of the English monarchs.

Arrangement:

1)   Alphabetical: no table of contents or index.
2)   Cross-references indicated by q. v. (quod vide, meaning

"which see").
3)   Appendices following dictionary proper.

Review Questions:

1)   For which of the following would you expect to find en-
     tries: Edgar Allan Poe, Mr. Micawber, Neoplatonism,
     Salome, sonnet, Cuchulain, Winston Churchill, Soren
     Kierkegaard, Robin Hood, Grub Street, Honoré de Balzac,
     Zeus, Buckingham Palace, the romantic movement, the
     Globe Theatre, Henry VIII, St. Nicholas' clerk, chap-
     book, Scottish Chaucerians, oxymoron, Gloriana, Thor,
     Squire Western?

2)   For which of the following would you expect to find plot
     summaries: Mary Shelley's Frankenstein, Beowulf,
     Pope's The Rape of the Lock, Shakespeare's Hamlet,
     Antonia Fraser's Mary Queen of Scots, Golding's Lord
     of the Flies?

Research Problems:

1)   Define and illustrate an anacrusis. Describe the two
     principal rhyme schemes of the sonnet. Describe the
     rhyme scheme and meter of the Spenserian stanza, and
     name four English poets who used this stanza form.

2)   What are Theophrastian "characters"? In which century
     did this form enjoy a vogue in England? What English
     character writer was murdered in the Tower of London?

3)   Explain the following expressions and their origins: to
     dine with Duke Humphrey, dandiprat, limehouse, to out-
     Herod Herod.

Notes (OCEL)

1.   For wider coverage of recent English authors, see Part
     II of Twentieth-Century British Literature (S7) and
     The New Century Handbook of English Literature (S4).
     Another alternative to the OCEL is The Penguin Com-
     panion to English Literature (S5). Also see The
     Reader's Encyclopedia of Shakespeare (S6).

2.   Since the OCEL only occasionally notes the "best and
     latest" editions of literary works, for fuller informa-

tion about standard editions, see Wright's A Reader's
Guide to English and American Literature (S2) or
Bateson's A Guide to English Literature (S3).
     A book-length chronological index of works is
provided by Annals of English Literature, 1475-1950:
The Principal Publications of Each Year, Together
with an Alphabetical Index of Authors with Their Works,
2nd ed. (Oxford: Clarendon Press, 1961). A brief
parallel outline of English and American literary history appears in Holman's A Handbook to Literature
(M9).

3. For allusions not explained in the OCEL, check Brewer's
    Dictionary of Phrase and Fable (S11), The Oxford
    Dictionary of English Proverbs (S14), a classical hand-
    book or dictionary (M11, S24, S25), and The Inter-
    preter's Dictionary of the Bible (S23). Also useful
    are Mythology of All Races (S85), Funk & Wagnalls
    Standard Dictionary of Folklore, Mythology and Legend
    (S12), Britannica (M36a), and specialized historical
    and biographical dictionaries such as Steinberg's Dic-
    tionary of British History (S34), An Encyclopedia of
    World History (S86), The Dictionary of National Bi-
    ography (M14), and Who's Who (M15).

4. For literary terms, also see Holman's A Handbook to
    Literature (M9), Shipley's Dictionary of World Liter-
    ary Terms (M10), Richard A. Lanham, A Handlist of
    Rhetorical Terms: A Guide for Students of English
    Literature (Berkeley: University of California Press,
    1969), and the Encyclopedia of Poetry and Poetics
    (S21).

M2. Hart, James D. The Oxford Companion to American
     Literature. 4th ed. New York: Oxford University
     Press, 1965.

     Aside from the inclusion of Canadian literature, the
OCAL is more circumscribed in its coverage than the OCEL:
few foreign entries appear. On the other hand, Hart provides
considerably more cultural, social, and political background
than does Harvey, thus reflecting the social-science orientation of many American literary studies.

Contents:

1) Authors: biographies and works with their dates;[1] data on foreign authors limited to their association with American literature.
2) Works: includes over a thousand summaries; some use of quotations.
3) Characters (fictional and historical).
4) Literary terms, other than standard prosodic ones.
5) Literary schools and movements; also entries for literary awards, literary societies, scholarly organizations, magazines, newspapers, anthologies, book collectors, printers, colleges and universities and their alumni in the world of letters.
6) Cultural background: "social, economic, aesthetic, scientific, military, political and religious figures and events that have affected the actions and thoughts, and hence the writings, in the lands now forming the United States..." (Preface).
7) Major literature of Canada. [2]
8) Appendix: Chronological Index of Literature and Social History 1578-1955.

Arrangement:

1) Alphabetical: no table of contents or index.
2) Cross-references indicated by q.v. (quod vide meaning "which see").
3) Appendix following dictionary proper.

Review questions:

1) For which of the following would you expect to find entries: Isadora Duncan, the Mennonites, blank verse, the Algonquin Indians, Shakespeare, the Wizard of Oz, Horatio Alger, The Saturday Evening Post, transcendentalism, World War II, the Beat movement, Ralph Ellison's Invisible Man, the detective story, T. S. Eliot, Sherwood Anderson, Leaves of Grass, Death of a Salesman, chantey, Shaw's Major Barbara, Captain Ahab, Holden Caulfield, Scrooge, Tom Sawyer, free verse, realism?

2) Describe the difference in emphasis between the OCEL and OCAL.

Research Problems:

1) What are "gift books"? When were they popular? In

what gift book were many of Hawthorne's Twice-Told
Tales first published? Which of these tales is a moral
allegory or parable dealing with man's isolation from his
fellows and from God?

2) Who were the major twentieth-century Agrarian writers?
In what did they believe? In what decades were they active?

3) When was the Evergreen Review founded, and who are
some of its frequent American and foreign contributors?

Notes (OCAL)

1. Also see American Authors and Books (S8), Contemporary Authors (M16), The Penguin Companion to American Literature (M12, headnote), and The Reader's
   Encyclopedia of American Literature (S9).

2. For more extensive coverage, see The Oxford Companion
   to Canadian History and Literature (M1, headnote).

M3. A Literary History of England. Ed. Albert C. Baugh.
     2nd ed. New York: Appleton, 1967.

Unlike a handbook, a literary history is chronologically arranged and deals in some depth with the backgrounds of
the various periods as well as with specific authors. A student wishing to acquaint himself with, say, Anglo-Saxon literature would find little to assist him in the OCEL--the subject is too broad for adequate treatment in a handbook.
Baugh is still the standard one-volume history of English literature, striking a nice balance between detail and interpretation. The attempt to memorize Baugh before taking a comprehensive examination has become virtually an academic tra-
dition!
Note that although the second edition of Baugh updates
the critical coverage through the mid-1960's, the literature
surveyed is still limited to pre-World War II writings.

Contents:

1) English literature from its beginnings to 1939. [1]

2) French and Latin works written in England during the medieval period.
3) Irish and Scottish writers.
4) Ample use of quotation.
5) Philological, political, economic, and social background.
6) Bibliographical footnotes to standard editions and to significant biographical, critical, and historical books and articles.

Arrangement:

1) Identification of contributors opposite title page. [2]
2) Table of Contents: divided into Books (corresponding to the main periods in English literature), Parts, and Chapters; the latter often bear such broad titles as "The Spirit of the Restoration," "Aestheticism and Decadence," etc.
3) List of Abbreviations of journals and other scholarly publications cited in the bibliographical footnotes, pp. xiv-xv.
4) Chronological survey by periods: the text proper.
5) Marginal subject headings on each page of the text.
6) Bibliographical as well as substantive footnotes on each page of the text; these bibliographical citations are to works written before 1948 (Baugh's first edition).
7) Bibliographical Supplement following p. 1605 (secondary works written through the mid-1960's): "Throughout the text of this book, a point • set beside a page number indicates that references to new critical material [after 1948] will be found under an identical paragraph/page number [set in boldface] in the BIBLIOGRAPHICAL SUPPLEMENT" (Guide to Reference Marks, Book I, Part I).
8) Index (to the text and to the Bibliographical Supplement): "In the Index, a number preceded by a [boldfaced] S indicates a paragraph/page number in the BIBLIOGRAPHICAL SUPPLEMENT" (Guide to Reference Marks). [3]

Review Questions:

1) How does the arrangement of Baugh differ from that of the OCEL? Under what circumstances would you be compelled to begin your research with Baugh?

2) Where can you find bibliographical information in Baugh?

3) From when to when does the second edition update the 1948 edition in regard to primary works (works by the literary author)? In regard to secondary works (works about the literary author)?

4) How can you find bibliographical entries in the Supplement that continue the bibliographical discussion in the text proper?

5) What else is treated in Baugh aside from strictly literary concerns?

Research Problems:

1) In what respect was England "unique in the Europe of the year 1000"? What four factors made it so?

2) What historical "laws" of civilization does Toynbee attempt to discover in his Studies of History? Who were "the Webbs," and what bearing on literature does their work have? Cite one secondary study dealing with the Webbs.

3) Who were the three great novelists of the mid-eighteenth century, and what was each one's special gift to fiction? What is the most comprehensive modern literary history dealing with prose fiction of the mid-eighteenth century? What major studies of the eighteenth-century novel appeared in the 1950's?

Notes (Baugh)

1. For coverage of British literature through the early 1960's, see Raymond Las Vergnas' Book VIII of Emile Legouis and Louis Cazamian, A History of English Literature, trans. Helen Douglas Irvine, rev. ed. (New York: Macmillan, 1964).

2. The two-volume A Critical History of English Literature (New York: Ronald Press, 1960), written entirely by David Daiches, amply realizes the author's hope "that the pattern which a single mind imposes on this vast material will make my account more lively and suggestive than the conscientious composite works of

reference by teams of experts..." (Preface).

Individual literary periods are given excellent book-length treatment in The Oxford History of English Literature, ed. F. P. Wilson and Bonamy Dobrée (Oxford: Clarendon Press, 1945--). Fourteen volumes are planned.

Also see G. M. Trevelyan, History of England, 3rd ed. (London: Longmans, Green, 1958); Ernest A. Baker, The History of the English Novel, 10 vols. 1924-39; rpt. with an 11th vol. by Lionel Stevenson (New York: Barnes and Noble, 1967); Lionel Stevenson, The English Novel: A Panorama (Boston: Houghton Mifflin, 1960); George Watson, The Literary Critics (S82); William K. Wimsatt, Jr. and Cleanth Brooks, Literary Criticism: A Short History (New York: Knopf, 1957); and Sir Ifor Evans, A Short History of English Drama, 2nd ed. rev. and enl. (Boston: Houghton Mifflin, 1965).

3. Confronted with both a table of contents and an index, the student may find it a good rule to use the former for locating discussions of broad subjects, the latter for locating specific information.

M4. Literary History of the United States: History. Ed. Robert E. Spiller et al. 4th ed., rev. New York: Macmillan, 1974.

Although the collaborative effort of over fifty scholars, [1] the LHUS is informed by a single unifying thesis dictating its scope--that "American literature differs from all the modern literatures of Europe in that it depends both upon an imported culture and upon the circumstances of a New World radically different in human experience from the Old..." (Address to the Reader). Accordingly, the LHUS is not just an account of American writers but in effect a cultural history of America, viewed through the lens of literature.

Contents:

1) American writers and their works from colonial times through the early 1970's.
2) Quotations from literary authors.
3) Broad cultural and historical chapters, e.g., "The

European Background, " "Literary Culture on the Fron-
tier, " "Literature as Business."
4) Bibliographical essays: a discursive introduction to
the most important primary and secondary works in
American literature; since this section is designed for
the general reader rather than the scholar, technical
and highly specialized studies are omitted.[2]

Arrangement:

1) Table of Contents: titles of cultural background chapters are italicized.
2) Eleven chapters divided into eighty-six sub-chapters,
each sub-chapter being a self-contained and eminently
readable essay by a major scholar.
3) Identification of contributors, pp. 1476-79.
4) Chronological survey by periods: the text proper.
5) Bibliography, pp. 1480-1520; after an introductory discussion of books of a general nature, the order of
bibliographical essays corresponds to the order of the
critical chapters.
6) Index: includes subjects, authors, and works; to some
extent, then, the LHUS can be used as a handbook.

Review Questions:

1) What are the main differences between the LHUS (Spiller)
and the OCAL?

2) Are the LHUS chapters signed?

3) Which of the following would you expect to find discussed:
science in America, the New Yorker magazine, Imagist
poetry, Calvinism, Davy Crockett, free speech, Alexander Hamilton, Dashiell Hammett, the labor movement,
Naturalism, Jewish-American literature, T. S. Eliot's
Four Quartets?

Research Problems:

1) Was Poe more appreciated by American or by foreign
writers? What Victorian poet thought Poe the most
original American genius? In what way was Poe's cen-
tral conception of art anti-romantic? Whose critical
insight is this? (That is, who wrote the chapter on Poe?)

2) What quality of American humor do foreigners consider

our greatest gift to literature? Cite the author and title
of the pioneer study of American humor.

3) With what subjects did Paul Goodman concern himself
    during the 1960's? Can you name another spokesman
    of the 1960's whose writings are considered to the
    left of Goodman's? Whose critical opinion are you
    following? Name a major work by this critic.

Notes (LHUS: History)

1. Cunliffe's The Literature of the United States (S83) is a
    one-author work treating American literature. Also
    see Quinn's The Literature of the American People
    (S84) and Wimsatt and Brooks' Literary Criticism: A
    Short History (M3, n. 2).

2. The guide to paperbound critical series (p. 1480) is of
    particular value to the student bent on acquiring his
    own library.

M5. The New Cambridge Bibliography of English Literature.
     Ed. George Watson [Vols. I-III] and I. R. Willi-
     son [Vol. IV]. Cambridge: Cambridge Univer-
     sity Press, 1969-74. (An index volume is forth-
     coming.)

     The New CBEL is the starting place for any serious
research into English literature.[1] This work is a vast--
though selective--primary and secondary bibliography; that
is, it lists works by the author and works about the author
and his canon. The New CBEL treats British writers whose
reputations were established by 1950; critical coverage for
all writers is now virtually up to date. Despite its modern-
ity, however, the New CBEL will never entirely supersede
its predecessor because it omits much of the intellectual,
political, and social background material included in F. W.
Bateson's great pioneer effort, the CBEL.[2]

Contents:

1) Writers native to or mainly resident in the British
    Isles.

2) Writers whose reputations were established by 1950;
also includes works written after 1950 by authors established prior to that date.

3) Primary bibliography of works in book form; generally
excludes short pamphlets and contributions to periodicals and miscellanies except in the case of the most
prominent literary figures. [3]

4) Primary bibliographies include works in both English
and Latin.

5) Indication of further unlisted works.

6) Intellectual, political, and social background:
   a. representative works by historians, theologians,
      philosophers, scholars, and scientists.
   b. representative ephemeral literature--i.e., political
      and controversial pamphlets, anonymous and pseu-
      donymous squibs, [4] mock-biographies, etc.
   c. representative literary bypaths--i.e., letter-writ-
      ing, sport, oratory, travel, and law.

7) History of printing and publishing; newspapers and
magazines

8) Manuscripts up to 1500 A.D.

9) First editions: number of volumes, place of publication (if other than London), date.

10) Dates of extant editions and translations up to fifty
years from the first.

11) Details of the more important or convenient modern
editions and reprints, both collected and individual.

12) Selected secondary books and articles in all languages
by critics of all nationalities. [5]

Arrangement:

1) Chronological: Vol. I--Anglo-Saxon, Middle English,
Renaissance to Restoration; Vol. II--Restoration to
Romantic Revival; Vol. III--the Nineteenth Century;
Vol. IV--The Twentieth Century.

2) Detailed Table of Contents for each volume.

3) List of Contributors and Abbreviations at front of each
volume.

4) General Introduction, Vol. I: bibliographies, histories,
anthologies, prosodic and linguistic studies.

5) Introductions to each period.

6) Sub-divisions into genres or literary topics within
each period, i.e., Fiction, Scottish Literature, etc.

7) Further subdivision into individual authors within each
genre: bibliographies, collected editions, separate
works, secondary studies; heading #1 denotes primary

bibliography, heading #2 secondary.

8) Primary bibliography--the author's canon--usually in a single chronological list.

9) Secondary bibliography for the entire canon in a single chronological list. [6]

10) Provisional indexes of primary authors and some subjects at the end of each volume. A master index volume is projected.

Review Questions:

1) To appear in the New CBEL, by what year must an author's reputation have been established?

2) Why is Bateson's CBEL still worth consulting?

3) Do American authors appear in the New CBEL? American critics?

4) Mention some off-literary subjects covered in the New CBEL.

5) In what part of the New CBEL can you find bibliographies of grammar, syntax, and vocabulary?

6) Under what period and subject headings would you expect to find the bibliography of Beowulf? Of the Globe playhouse?

7) Would you find an entry for Paradise Lost in the Index?

Research Problems:

1) What is the subject of Stephen Gosson's The Schoole of Abuse? When was it first printed? Cite another work by Gosson. How many editions of this work were published in the sixteenth century?

2) Cite an anthology devoted to five plays by Peter Ustinov. Which plays does it contain? How many unpublished plays has Ustinov written? Cite a critical work on Ustinov.

3) Who translated Henryson's The Testament of Cresseid into modern English in 1945? In what work does E. M. W. Tillyard discuss The Testament?

Notes (New CBEL)

1. Also see Howard-Hill's Bibliography of British Literary
    Bibliographies (S42), Shakespearian Bibliography and
    Textual Criticism (S42, passim), and Thompson's
    Motif-Index of Folk Literature (S13).
        For the comparative literature counterpart of
    the New CBEL, see Baldensperger and Friedrich's
    Bibliography of Comparative Literature (S57).

2. The Cambridge Bibliography of English Literature, ed.
    F. W. Bateson, 4 vols. (Cambridge: Cambridge Uni-
    versity Press, 1940); and Supplement: A. D. 600-
    1900 [Vol. V of CBEL], ed. George Watson (Cam-
    bridge: Cambridge University Press, 1957. The orig-
    inal work included the literatures of India, South Afri-
    ca, Canada, Australia, and New Zealand as well as
    background bibliographies on science, economics, law,
    and classical and oriental scholarship. However,
    other extra-literary sections have been retained and
    updated. Note that the 1900-1950 volume contains ex-
    tensive material on book production and distribution,
    theatre as a mass media, writers on off-literary sub-
    jects, and newspapers and magazines.

3. Keep in mind that despite their size, both the CBEL and
    New CBEL are selective bibliographies. The list of
    works by a minor author may not always be complete.
    Moreover, entries for works by a minor author may
    be dispersed under various headings without cross-
    references, making the use of indexes essential.

4. For anonyma and pseudonyma, also see Halkett and
    Laing's Dictionary (S1), the National Union Catalog
    (M23), the British Museum General Catalogue (S52),
    and Pollard and Redgrave's Short-Title Catalogue
    (M24), including those works listed under M24, n. 2
    which comprise the English national bibliography.

5. For biography, also consult the Dictionary of National
    Biography (M14).

6. Unfortunately, secondary material is not classified ac-
    cording to the particular primary work or subject
    treated, as was the editorial practice for the CBEL;
    for example, in order to find studies dealing with

"In Memoriam, " one must scan all nineteen pages
of Tennyson criticism.

M6.   Literary History of the United States: Bibliography.
         Ed. Robert Spiller et al.   4th ed., rev. New
         York: Macmillan, 1974.

    The LHUS: Bibliography contains discursive, selec-
tive primary and secondary bibliographies of books, periodical items, monograph studies, technical and textual studies,
and bibliographies for the specialist--all integrally related
to the discussions in the LHUS: History. "They are intended as a guide to the present state of resources and
scholarship in American literary culture. Though descriptive in nature, they constitute a factual history in which a
theory of criticism is implicit in the arrangement" (Preface).
    To use the LHUS: Bibliography and its incorporated
supplements with facility, one should know something about
Spiller's successive additions. The original bibliography
was published in 1948. In 1959 the first bibliographical supplement appeared covering the decade 1948-58; in 1972 Supplement II appeared covering 1959 through 1970. The fourth
revised edition of the LHUS: Bibliography, while one inclusive volume, is only partially cumulated. Although the volume has a single table of contents and index and is contin-
uously paginated, it is still arranged in the order of its initial compilation: the first supplement follows the original
work; the second supplement follows the first.

Contents:

1) Coverage through 1970, in some cases 1971.
2) Guide to Resources: library holdings in American
     literary culture throughout the U.S., catalogs, direc-
     tories, union lists, special collections; guides to ref-
     erence books, theses, and other professional studies;
     registries of publication of books, periodicals, and
     newspapers; biographical and reference dictionaries
     and digests; sources for cultural history.
3) Bibliographies of Literature and Culture: general--
     periodicals, clubs, histories, movements; specific--
     by period and type (colonial through twentieth cen-
     tury); folk literature; Indian lore; popular litera-
     ture.
4) Movements and Influences: literature of travel and
     westward migration; non-English writing in America;

      regionalism and local color throughout the U.S.; science and social criticism; literature of slavery and the Civil War; transcendentalism and utopianism; escapism and aestheticism; American writers and books abroad.

5)   Bibliographies of authors: information on separate and collected works, edited texts and reprints, biography and criticism, primary sources (including manuscript location in public depositories), and secondary bibliographies; primary sources are selective with respect to separates, magazine pieces, and ephemera. [1]

Arrangement:

1)   Cumulated, detailed Table of Contents: pp. xi-xxvii.
2)   Key to Abbreviations: pp. xi-xxvii.
3)   The 1948 bibliography: pp. 3-790, followed by
4)   The 1959 bibliography: pp. 793-1033, followed by
5)   The 1972 bibliography: pp. 1037-1375.
6)   Cumulated index: at end of second supplement, pp. 1377-1466. Entries for names of literary authors, major critics, titles, and subjects;[2] cross-references in both index and text.

Review Questions:

1)   How do the bibliographies found here differ from those at the end of the LHUS: History? In what ways are the bibliographical treatments similar?

2)   Until what year does the fourth revised edition of LHUS: Bibliography extend its coverage?

3)   What is meant by a "Guide to Resources"?

4)   Why are three page references often given for a subject in the table of contents?

Research Problems:

1)   What general holdings of the Henry E. Huntington

Library in San Marino, California would interest a
researcher concerned with American literary culture?
Name a work by a major nineteenth-century New
England writer that was edited in 1960 from a manuscript in the Huntington Library. Name a directory that indexes special collections in libraries
throughout the United States and that is regularly revised and updated.

2) List three recent (1970-71) comprehensive bibliog-
raphies of black history and culture in America.
Cite a compilation of black songs of World War I.
In what work can you find evaluations by black writ-
ers of William Styron's The Confessions of Nat
Turner?

3) Cite two twentieth-century studies of women's education in the nineteenth century. Cite three anthologies compiled in the nineteenth century of American
women writers. Evaluate the LHUS bibliographical
coverage of women's achievements and problems, literary and other, in the twentieth century.

Notes (LHUS: Bibliography)

1. Also see Blanck's Bibliography of American Literature (M22), Nilon's Bibliography of Bibliographies
in American Literature (S43), Leary's Articles on
American Literature (S49a, S49b), American Literary Scholarship (S48), Dissertations in American
Literature (M27, n.1), Woodress' Eight American
Authors and Bryer's Sixteen Modern American Authors (S50), Ghodes' Bibliographical Guide (S47),
Jones and Ludwig's Guide (S10), the MLA International Bibliography (M7), American Literature's
and American Quarterly's serial bibliographies
(M19), and "the continuing bibliographies in such
journals as ... American Historical Review, Amer-
ican Studies, Bulletin of the British Association
for American Studies, Newsletter of the European
Association for American Studies, Jahrbuch für
Amerikastudien, and Studi Americani" (Suppl. II,
Preface).
For the comparative literature counterpart of

the LHUS: Bibliography, see Baldensperger and
Friederich's Bibliography of Comparative Literature
(S57).

2.   "For each author who is given an individual bibliography, the main entry is italicized.   These authors are indicated by an asterisk before the surname" (Index).

M7.   MLA International Bibliography of Books and Articles
on the Modern Languages and Literatures.   New
York: Modern Language Association of America,
1922--.

At present, the MLA International Bibliography is
an annual, non-cumulative catalog of secondary works only,
by critics of all nationalities about literary authors of all
nationalities.   Its functions are 1) to update other bibliographies and 2) to provide near-comprehensive secondary
coverage.

First published in 1922 as part of the scholarly
journal PMLA (Publications of the Modern Language Association of America), it was originally called "American
Bibliography" because only American scholarship was entered.   The bibliography for 1956, still part of PMLA,
appeared under a new title, "Annual Bibliography," to re-
flect a major policy change: the listing of secondary works
by scholars of all nationalities.   The current title dates
from the bibliography for 1963.   With the bibliography
for 1969, the MLA International Bibliography assumed its
current format of four annual volumes, independent of PMLA.[1]
The new format is described below with emphasis on Volume
I, which includes studies of English and American literature; bibliographies for earlier years differ in both subjects covered and in details of arrangement.

Contents:

1)   Subject coverage: Vol. I. General, English, American, Medieval and Neo-Latin, and Celtic literatures;
Vol. II.   European, Asian, African, and Latin-Amer-
ican literatures; Vol. III.   Linguistics; IV.   Pedagogy
in the modern foreign languages.

2)   Secondary works only: articles, essays, monographs, book-length studies; scholarly editions and anthologies are, however, included.
3)   Scholars of all nationalities represented.
4)   Annual Listings: coverage of current scholarship within two years; items received after mid-January are entered in the following year's issue. [2]

Arrangement:

1)   Table of Contents.
2)   List of Abbreviations.
3)   Catalog style: unannotated entries (after early issues) except for titles requiring explanation. [3]
4)   Main divisions of Vol. I: Festschriften and other analyzed collections;[4] general literature, literary criticism, aesthetics, etc.; English literature; American literature; Latin literature; Celtic literature.
5)   Subdivisions within the national literatures: first by period, then alphabetically by author.
6)   Itemized entries: each entry is preceded by an Arabic item number, essential for the use of the index and for cross-reference. Note that volume numbers of journals appear in Arabic numerals and that un-dated items are understood to have been published in the years of the bibliography.
7)   Intra-volume cross-references: these are found at the ends of the sections or sub-sections, appearing as a series of item numbers.
8)   Index: From 1964 on, found at the end of each volume; lists contributors' names only, followed by the item numbers of their works.
9)   Non-cumulative issues.

Review Questions:

1)   How often does the MLA International Bibliography appear? Is it cumulative? Is it annotated? In what sense was it always "international"? Why was it called "American Bibliography" prior to 1956?

2)   Which volume of the new four-volume MLA International Bibliography is of interest to students of American Literature? To students of Comparative Literature?

3)   For which of the following would you expect to find entries: a collection of critical essays on Christian literary

criticism, an unedited commercial reprint of An American Tragedy, an English translation of Icelandic poetry,
an article on the etymology of "mumbo-jumbo"? Would
you expect to find a listing of works by Ernest Heming-
way?

4) How does the MLA International Bibliography supplement
   the New CBEL and the LHUS: Bibliography?

5) What are the basic classifications within the field of English literature?

6) How can you ascertain how prolific a particular scholar
   is?

Research Problems:

1) How many entries for Hamlet do you find in the PMLA
   American Bibliography for 1921? In the 1967 MLA International Bibliography? Suggest one factor to account
   for the increase. How does the style of the 1921 bibliography differ from that of the bibliographies of the
   1960's?

2) List the English language articles published in 1967 on
   Paul Valéry. (Explain all title abbreviations).

3) Discover what is discussed in the following articles without consulting the articles themselves:
   Alspach, Russell K. "Two Songs of Yeats," MLN, 61
   (1946), 395-400. Swanson, Carl A. "Ibsen and the
   Comédie-Française." SS 19 (1946), 70-78.

Notes (MLA)

1. The 1921-1968 bibliographies have been reprinted under
   separate cover by the Kraus Reprint Corporation and
   by New York University Press.

2. Thus, to prepare a complete listing of works published
   in 1965, the student would have to consult both the
   bibliographies for 1965 and 1966; he might consult the
   1967 bibliography as well, since occasionally a work
   will elude the bibliographer for even longer then one
   year. For complete and current coverage, he might
   also check the MLA International Bibliography's

British counterpart, Annual Bibliography of English
Language and Literature (S44).   Also see The Year's
Work in English Studies (S45); The Year's Work in
Modern Language Studies (S59); Index to Little Maga-
zines (S70); Index to Commonwealth Little Magazines
(S71); Social Sciences and Humanities Index (S68);
British Humanities Index (S69); Essay and General
Literature Index (M28); and the most recent of the
specialized bibliographies appearing in scholarly peri-
odicals (M19).   With regard to the last, note that
American Literature publishes its bibliography quarter-
ly.

3.   However, from 1971 on, an asterisk after an entry indicates that a 200-word abstract of that article will be
found in MLA Abstracts (S66).   For other abstracts
of current criticism, see entries in Chapter IV.

4.   A Festschrift is an anthology of essays offered as a
tribute to an eminent scholar.   An analyzed collection
is one whose contents are described on its Library of
Congress card.

M8.   The Oxford English Dictionary.   Ed.   James A. H.
Murray et al.   13 vols.   1933; rpt. Oxford: Oxford University Press, 1961.

As the running title indicates, the OED is "a Corrected
Re-Issue with an Introduction, Supplement, and Bibliography
of a New English Dictionary on Historical Principles [NED]
... [1888-1928]. "   From its inception to the completion of
the thirteenth volume (the OED will be a sixteen-volume work
when its current supplement is completed), half a century's
labor was well expended.   "Murray's" is a remarkable
achievement, tracing the history of "the words that have
formed the English vocabulary from the time of the earliest
records down to the present day, with all relevant facts concerning their form, sense-history, pronunciation, and etymology" (Preface).   Dated quotations with exact bibliographical references illustrate each change of meaning.   Volumes
I through XII constitute the dictionary proper.   Volume XIII
is the 1933 supplement.

Contents (Vols. I-XII):

1) Standard works: current, obsolete (unless obsolete by
   1150), archaic.
2) The main technical vocabulary of the English language.
3) Some dialect (especially before 1500) and slang.
4) Dated quotations illustrating changes in meaning.

Arrangement:

1) General Explanations: especially important is the material on Classification of the Vocabulary (I, xxviii-
   xxxiv).
2) List of Abbreviations, Signs, &c. precedes "A" entries.
3) Dictionary proper: division into main words (in bold
   type), subordinate words, or combinations; these are
   listed in a single alphabet with subordinate words (usually variant or obsolete forms) and combinations con-
   cluding the main entry.
4) Identification of each main entry word: main form,
   pronunciation, part of speech, specification by field
   to which it is related (e.g., music, astronomy), status
   (colloquial, dialectal, etc.), spelling history, inflec-
   tion.
5) Morphology (form history): etymology, subsequent
   change, miscellaneous historical facts.
6) Definitions and quotations.

Contents and Arrangement (Vol. XIII):

1) New words and new senses of old words noted between
   the 1880's and 1930's. [1]
   a. Selective, not exhaustive. [2]
   b. More citations from American usage.
   c. More proper names.
2) Additions and Emendations: corrections based on
   further research, errata, mostly earlier examples.
3) List of Spurious Words.
4) List of Books Quoted (the "Bibliography"): fuller entries (author, title, date) for quotations in the main
   dictionary.

Review Questions:

1) What unique feature of the OED distinguishes it from
   other dictionaries?

2) Why is it necessary to always check both the Supplement and the Additions and Emendations when looking up recent or early meanings and recorded usage?

3) What is a spurious word?

4) Quotations from most of Christopher Marlowe's works are cited in the OED. In consequence, would the list of Books Quoted enumerate his entire canon?

Research Problems:

1) Define "blarney" as a transitive and as an intransitive verb. What is its origin and status? What is the first recorded example of its use? (Note author's name—given as well as surname—work, dates of composition and publication).

2) Gloss the italicized works: "Away you Scullion ... I'le tickle your catastrophe."

3) What is the full title of the work in which "gaol" was first used as a transitive verb meaning to confine in a jail?

Notes (OED)

1. A new updating has been in progress for the last fifteen years. R. W. Burchfield's A Supplement to the Oxford English Dictionary, Vol. I, covering A-G, was released by Oxford University Press in 1972. The two final volumes are expected by 1977. Slang—American, sexual, etc.—holds a much larger place in this Supplement than in the previous work.

2. Additional coverage is provided by Words and Phrases Index: A Guide to Antedatings, New Words, New Compounds, New Meanings, and Other Published Scholarship Supplementing the Oxford English Dictionary, Dictionary of Americanisms, Dictionary of American English and Other Major Dictionaries of the English Language, comp. C. Edward Wall and Edward Przebienda (Ann Arbor: Pierian Press, 1969—). Since the WPI merely locates scholarly discussions of words, the user must also consult the periodical sources to which he is referred.

The student may wish to purchase the one-volume Shorter Oxford English Dictionary on Historical Principles, ed. William Little et al., 3rd ed. (1944; rpt. with corrections Oxford: Clarendon Press, 1962). For those whom only the original can satisfy, a "micrographic" (photographically shrunk) two-volume Compact OED, complete with magnifying glass, has been available since 1971. Also see The American Heritage Dictionary (S28), Webster's New Dictionary of Synonyms (S29), A Dictionary of American-English Usage (S30), The Careful Writer (S31), Eric A. Partridge, A Dictionary of Slang and Unconventional English: Colloquialisms and Catch-Phrases, Solecisms and Catachreses, Nicknames, Vulgarisms, and such Americanisms as have been Naturalized, 7th ed., Supplement rev. and enl. 2 vols. (London: Routledge and Kegan Paul, [1970]), and Maxim Newmark, Dictionary of Foreign Words (Paterson, N.J.: Littlefield, Adams, 1962).

CHAPTER II

DICTIONARIES, HANDBOOKS, AND GUIDES

M9. A Handbook to Literature

M10. Dictionary of World Literary Terms

M11. The Oxford Classical Dictionary

M12. Penguin Companion to Literature: European

M13. Guide to Reference Books

M14. Dictionary of National Biography

M15. Who's Who

M16. Contemporary Authors

     Chapter II introduces a number of works dealing with literary terms, foreign literature, reference tools, and biography. All but Winchell's Guide to Reference Books are alphabetically arranged and, consequently, can be used with ease. One cannot, however, stress Winchell's value too strongly; familiarity with this Guide is as rewarding to students of literature as to librarians. The last three entries have been chosen for the way in which each answers a special need. Capsule biographies of well-known figures can be found in handbooks and encyclopedias; full-length biographies can be located through bibliographies. But for extensive scholarly biographical sketches of Britishers no longer living, the DNB is unrivaled. Who's Who and Contemporary Authors, the former mainly British in coverage, the latter American, are especially valuable for their biographical data on figures not yet sufficiently famous to have become the subject of a "life."

M9. Holman, C. Hugh. A Handbook to Literature: Based

on the Original by William Flint Thrall and Addi-
son Hibbard.   3rd ed.   Indianapolis: Odyssey
Press, 1972.

This is the latest revision of the 1936 "Thrall and
Hibbard, " the standard literary handbook used in American
universities.   The orientation is both critical and historical
with entries for "words and phrases peculiar to [but not necessarily limited to] the study of English and American literature. " Holman makes an inexpensive, worthwhile addition to
one's personal library; the omitted information--biographies,
plot summaries, and characters--is easily accessible else-
where.

Contents:

1) Literary terms, many from classical rhetoric.
2) Literary forms.
3) Some common literary allusions (though not nearly as
    many as are found in the OCEL).
4) Literary schools and movements.
5) Major literary periodicals and prizes.
6) Chronological outline of English and American literary
    history, entered side by side, to facilitate comparison
    between the two literatures.
7) Appendices: National Book Awards for Fiction, Poetry,
    Arts and Letters; Nobel Prizes for Literature; Pulitzer
    Prizes for Fiction, Poetry, and Drama.

Arrangement:

1) Alphabetical; no Table of Contents or Index.
2) Cross-references: in small capitals in the body of
    the article; preceded by "See ... " at the end of the
    article.
3) Explanations of abbreviations used in the chronological
    outline, p. 561.

Review Questions:

1) Does Holman provide biographical entries? Entries for
    individual works?

2) What reference work supplements Holman's chronological
    outline of American literary history with an outline of
    political and scientific events?

3)   For which of the following would you expect to find en-
     tries: existential criticism, erotic literature, dead
     metaphor, frontier literature, sonnet, The Dial (a peri-
     odical featuring American transcendentalist works)?

Research Problems:

1)   Which English literary works were published in the fol-
     lowing years: 1557, 1638, 1846? What great Anglo-
     American writer died in 1965?

2)   What is a "curtal sonnet"? Describe its form and rhyme
     scheme. Name a well-known curtal sonnet.

3)   Explain the nature of the "profile" as a literary type.
     Where did the term originate?

M10. Dictionary of World Literary Terms: Forms, Tech-
      nique, Criticism. Ed. Joseph T. Shipley. Rev.
      and enl. Boston: The Writer, 1970.

        Unlike Holman, entries in Shipley are drawn from all
literatures, many entries are of substantial length, and valuable essay-surveys of American, European, and Classical
criticism are included. Shipley, then, may be regarded as
an excellent supplement to Holman, particularly for the study
of world literature and criticism. [1]

Contents:

1)   Definitions of literary terms (forms, techniques,
     schools, movements, ideas) from all literatures
     and periods; where appropriate, the history of the
     term is discussed and examples of its use are
     provided.
2)   Short bibliographies appended to many articles.
3)   Surveys of literary criticism in America, England,
     France, Germany, Greece, Italy, Russia, and Spain;
     also surveys of Latin (Roman) criticism and medieval
     criticism.
4)   Many signed articles by recognized authorities.
5)   List of foreign critics and their works; major Euro-
     pean literatures are not represented.

Arrangement:

1) Abbreviations and symbols found in the articles, pp. xi-xiii.
2) Part I. Dictionary: alphabetical entries of literary terms; numerous cross-references.
3) Part II. Critical Surveys: arranged first by country, then by period.
4) Part III. Selected List of Critics and Works: devoted to countries not covered in Part II; under the national heading, arranged chronologically.

Review Questions:

1) For which of the following would you expect to find entries: parody, Francesco Petrarch, Petrarchism, fable, Lysistrata, Nō drama, livre à clef?

2) Aside from the basic dictionary entries, what features does Shipley contain?

Research Problems:

1) Who originated the term "Theatre of Cruelty"? How does modern theatre of cruelty differ from the nineteenth-century French Grand Guignol play? Cite a work dealing with theatre of cruelty in French literature.

2) Who is frequently regarded as the first American science fiction writer? What is "social science fiction"? Who is the critic you are quoting? Cite four anti-utopian literary works written in the twentieth century. What is H. Bruce Franklin's contribution to the subject of utopian fiction?

3) What is an "aptronym"? Cite examples from Homer, Spenser, and Restoration drama.

Notes (Shipley)

1. For foreign literature, Shipley can be best used in conjunction with the Penguin Companion to Literature (M12), Benét's Reader's Encyclopedia (S15), The Reader's Encyclopedia of World Drama (S19), Modern World Theater (S20), The Oxford Companion to French Literature (S27), The Oxford Classical Dictionary

(M11), The New Century Classical Handbook (S24),
and The Oxford Companion to Classical Literature
(S25).

An outstanding work, similar to Shipley but re-
stricted to poetry, is the Encyclopedia of Poetry and
Poetics (S21). For English and American literary
criticism, see Watson's The Literary Critics (S82)
and Wimsatt and Brooks' Literary Criticism: A Short
History (M3, n. 2).

M11. The Oxford Classical Dictionary. Ed. N. G. L. Ham-
         mond and H. H. Scullard. 2nd ed. Oxford:
         Clarendon Press, 1970.

The OCD is a fairly recondite reference tool, featur-
ing signed scholarly articles (many of which are extensive
surveys rather than capsule summaries) and concise appended
bibliographies. Although all aspects of classical civilization
are covered, the emphasis is upon literature and biography.
For the student with little Latin and less Greek, the OCD
might best be used in conjunction with the New Century Classical Handbook (S24) or The Oxford Companion to Classical
Literature (S25).

Contents:

1)   Greek and Roman civilization from Greek pre-history
     through the death of the Emperor Constantine in 337
     A.D. (with a few later entries).
2)   Mythological and legendary figures and places. [1]
3)   Accounts of historical peoples and persons (including
     leading Christians). [2]
4)   Literary forms and writers; works not separately en-
     tered. [3]
5)   Festivals, customs, art, etc.
6)   Places of legendary, historical, and archaeological
     interest.
7)   Bibliographies appended to many articles.
8)   A General Bibliography.

Arrangement:

1)   Signs and Abbreviations, pp. [ix]-xii: important for
     references to authors and books, both ancient and
     modern.

2)   Dictionary proper: alphabetically arranged.
3)   Appendix: General Bibliography, pp. 1151-53.
4)   Index of Names, etc. which are not titles of dictionary entries, pp. [1154]-73.
5)   Index to initials of contributors, pp. [1174]-76.

Review Questions:

1)   For which of these would you expect to find entries: Atlantis, Alexander the Great, Medical Science in Classical Greece, Greek allegory, Cleopatra, Aphrodite, Woden, Abraham?

2)   Under what subject heading would you look for an account of Circe, the enchantress in The Odyssey?

3)   Would you expect to find a detailed plot summary of Aristophanes' play Lysistrata?

4)   Are articles in the OCD signed? Are bibliographies appended? Is there an index?

Research Problems:

1)   How does Caesar depict himself in De Bello Gallico and De Bello Civili? Describe the style of the Commentaries. Who wrote the article from which you are quoting?

2)   What was the tyrant Dionysius' most successful literary work? What literary relics did Dionysius possess?

3)   Where was the probable location of the sanctuary in which the Lenaea was celebrated? What was the chief importance of this festival? Cite an English-language work in which the Lenaea is discussed.

Notes (OCD)

1.   Also see Graves' The Greek Myths (S26) and The Mythology of All Races (S85).

2.   For further coverage, see The Encyclopedia of World Art (S92), The Encyclopedia of Philosophy (S88), The Encyclopaedia of Religion and Ethics (S89), The New Catholic Encyclopedia (S90), and The Encyclopedia Judaica (S91).

Those interested in the Bible as literature will wish to become familiar with The New Oxford Annotated Bible (S22) and The Interpreter's Dictionary of the Bible (S23).

3. Major literary works are entered and summarized in The New Century Classical Handbook (S24) and in The Oxford Companion to Classical Literature (S25). Also see Cassell's Encyclopedia of World Literature (S16), Benét's The Reader's Encyclopedia (S15), The Oxford Companion to the Theatre (S18), The Reader's Encyclopedia of World Drama (S19), and The Encyclopedia of Poetry and Poetics (S21).

4. For English-language criticism of classical writers, see Thomas Gwinup and Fidelia Dickinson, Greek and Roman Authors: A Checklist of Criticism (Metuchen, N.J.: Scarecrow Press, 1973).

M12.   The Penguin Companion to Literature: European.
        Vol. II. Ed. Anthony Thorlby. Harmondsworth, Middlesex: Penguin Books, 1969.

This is the second volume of a recent four-volume series covering world literature, the other titles being The Penguin Companion to Literature: Classical and Byzantine, Oriental and African, ed. D. R. Dudley and D. M. Lang (1969); The Penguin Companion to Literature: English and Commonwealth, ed. David Daiches (1971); and The Penguin Companion to American Literature, ed. Malcolm Bradbury, Eric Mottram and Jean Franco (1971). (This last work includes the literatures of Latin America.) The series is published in both hard and paper cover. Despite the limited kinds of entries (mostly by author's name only), the Penguin Companions are good buys.

Contents:

1) Entries primarily for literary authors with brief biographies; also some philosophers, historians, etc.
2) Fifth century A. D. to present.
3) Main works briefly described.
4) Available editions and translations. [1]
5) Selected criticism.

6)   Some entries for movements, anonymous works,
      classes of literature (Latin hymns), anonymous writ-
      ers (the Archpoet), literature of certain periods (Ru-
      manian literature before 1850), and literary types
      (Bildungs-roman). [2]

Arrangement:

1)   Identification of contributors, pp. 11-15: their initials
      appear in brackets at the end of their articles and be-
      fore the bibliography.
2)   Abbreviations of titles of books and articles cited in
      the bibliographies.
3)   Alphabetical entries; articles are followed by bibliog-
      raphies in small type. If a two-paragraph bibliography,
      the first paragraph lists editions and translations not
      given in the article itself, the second lists selected
      criticism.
4)   Cross-reference indicated by an arrow; multiple cross-
      references by a double arrow.
5)   Guide to Entries by Language and Country: alphabetical
      list by language in which the author wrote, not by
      his country of origin.   (Thus, Ionesco is listed under
      France, having written in French, and not under Ru-
      mania where he was born.) Note that all Albanian
      writers are followed by all Austrian writers, etc.
      Within the country, listing is chronological. The list-
      ing entry also gives the author's birth and death dates
      and his profession (if other than literature) or literary
      specialization.

Review Questions:

1)   What major feature of The Penguin Companion cannot be
      found in Shipley?

2)   For which of the following would you expect to find en-
      tries: Cervantes, Solzhenitsyn, Pushkin, Virgil, Swiss-
      German dialect literature, expressionism, Montesquieu,
      French literary criticism, Whitman, Omar Khayyam,
      Samuel Beckett?

3)   What kind of bibliographical aid is provided by the Pen-
      guin Companions?

4)   Are authors listed alphabetically in the Guide to Entries?

Research Problems:

1) What are Marie de France's Le Fresne and Lanval about? Whose illegitimate daughter could Marie de France have been? Whose half-sister? What is her importance for French literature? Name the critic you are following.

2) With what non-German modern writer has Günter Grass most often been compared? What work by this writer was published in the same year that Grass published Die Blechtrommel? How does the drum operate in this novel? Cite two critical works of the mid-1960's in which Grass is discussed.

3) When did Isaak Babel produce most of his work? What is the Konarmiya about? What are the characteristics of his style? Why is the date of his death uncertain? Cite the English translation of his stories.

Notes (Penguin)

1. For a more extensive listing of translations, see The Literatures of the World in English Translation (M21), Index Translationum (S77), and Yearbook of Comparative and General Literature (S58).

2. For subjects lending themselves to a comparative literature approach, see Bibliography of Comparative Literature (S57), Yearbook of Comparative and General Literature (S58), and the Dictionary of the History of Ideas (S33). Other works with foreign coverage include the Encyclopedia of Poetry and Poetics (S21), Motif-Index of Folk Literature (S13), Benét's Reader's Encyclopedia (S15), Cassell's Encyclopedia of World Literature (S16), The Oxford Companion to the Theatre (S18), Modern World Theatre (S20), Reader's Encyclopedia of World Drama (S19), Encyclopedia of World Literature in the 20th Century (S17), The Oxford Companion to French Literature (S27), The Oxford Classical Dictionary (M11), The New Century Classical Handbook (S24), The Oxford Companion to Classical Literature (S25), and Chambers's Biographical Dictionary (S41).

M13.   Winchell, Constance M. Guide to Reference Books.
       8th ed. Chicago: American Library Association,
       1967. (Biennial Supplements. Ed. Eugene P.
       Sheehy. Chicago: American Library Association,
       1968---.)

      Winchell--a selective annotated bibliography of refer-
ence works--is a goldmine. The listings of major resources
are comprehensive, accurate, and evaluative; the introductions to classes of reference works are exercises in lucidity.
This is the most helpful work to consult for general reference questions. By using Sheehy's supplements in conjunction with Winchell, the student can keep abreast of all major
reference publications.

Contents:

   1)   General commentary on classes of reference works.
   2)   Basic general and specialized reference books in all
        areas.
   3)   Works in foreign languages as well as in English. 1
   4)   Generally through 1964; first supplement: items pub-
        lished during 1965-66; second supplement: 1967-68;
        etc.
   5)   Full publishing information; description of contents,
        special features (e.g., indexes, bibliographies), dif-
        ference between new and older editions, etc.
   6)   Biennial supplements include Library of Congress
        card number for each entry; references to reviews
        often follow the annotations.

Arrangement:

   1)   Table of Contents, pp. ix-xii.
   2)   Principal abbreviations, p. xix.
   3)   Basic subject divisions:
        Part A.   General Reference Works.
        Part B.   The Humanities.
        Part C.   Social Sciences.
        Part D.   History and Area Studies.
        Part E.   Pure and Applied Sciences.
   4)   Catagories: found within many subject divisions and
        subdivisions in the following order:
        a.   guides and manuals.
        b.   bibliographies.
        c.   indexes and abstract journals.
        d.   encyclopedias.

       e.   dictionaries of special terms.
       f.   handbooks.
       g.   annuals and directories.
       h.   histories.
       i.   biographical works.
       j.   atlases.
       k.   serial publications.

5) "Whenever subdivisions by countries are used, the United States is listed first, with other countries following in alphabetical order" (Preface--Arrangement).

6) Cross-reference by code number.

7) Index includes author, subject, and some title entries. (References to code numbers followed by "n" refer to titles in annotations.)

8) Index to biennial Supplement I at end of that volume; cumulative index to successive biennial Supplements at end of each Supplement.

Review Questions:

1) Which of the following would you expect to find described in Winchell or in its Supplements: a German language bibliography of music, a handbook to civil engineering, an encyclopedia of Yucatan history, a journal of Soviet periodical abstracts?

2) Does Winchell describe new editions of older reference works? Are reviews of the reference works located?

3) What code letter distinguishes reference works on the humanities?

4) Are all titles described listed in the indexes?

5) Where are the indexes to the Supplements?

Research Problems:

1) Cite the most comprehensive collection of literary parodies in English. Is there an anthology devoted to parodies of twentieth-century American and British literature?

2) List four unabridged general French-English dictionaries suitable for American students.

3) Cite three English language reference works on occultism. Which one is multi-volumed, and how is it indexed?

Notes (Winchell)

1. Winchell's British counterpart is Walford's Guide to Reference Material (S35), which includes more foreign and fewer American works.

M14. The Dictionary of National Biography. Ed. Sir Leslie Stephen and Sir Sidney Lee. 63 vols. 1885-1901; rpt. in 21 vols. London: Oxford University Press, 1921-22.

Vol. XXII [First] Supplement. 1901; rpt. London: Oxford, 1959-60.

The Twentieth Century D. N. B. 6 vols. London: Oxford, 1912-71 (Continuing decennial supplements).

Corrections and Additions to the Dictionary of National Biography. Boston, Mass.: G. K. Hall, 1966.

The DNB is the classic source for British biography, as monumental a work in its field as the OED and the New CBEL are in theirs. The biographies are scholarly and extensive, biographies of minor figures are abundant, and the appended bibliographies are an additional useful feature. For the student who lacks time to read a full-length "life," the DNB is the best substitute.

The dictionary proper (Volumes I-XXI) is described below in detail. Additions to the DNB are described only with regard to their notable differences from the original volumes.

Contents (Vols. I-XXI).

1) Biographies of notable British subjects[1] (and rulers, listed under their Christian names) from the earliest times, and now deceased: includes early settlers in America, Britishers who gained fame abroad, and persons of foreign birth who gained fame in Britain.

2) Those who died prior to January 22, 1901 (Queen Victoria's death date), arranged in a single alphabet.

3) Legendary British figures (e.g., Robin Hood).

4) Signed articles by experts, with sources of information (often personal) cited.

5)   Bibliographies (bracketed) following each article.

Arrangement:

1)   List of Contributors to Vols. I-XXII (note that this includes the first Supplement): I, xi-xx.
2)   Index to each volume at the end of the respective volume. Birth and death dates as well as page numbers are given.
3)   Additional lives to be found in the first Supplement (Vol. XXII) are noted at the bottom of each page of each index, in the appropriate alphabetical place.

Contents and Arrangement (Suppl. --Vol. XXII)

1)   Those who died prior to January 22, 1901, but were excluded from their proper place in Vols. I-XXI, either because they died too late (publication extended over a fifteen-year period) or because they were accidentally omitted.
2)   Arranged in its own single alphabet.
3)   Its own index at end.

Contents and Arrangement (20th Century DNB):

1)   Six decennial volumes to date:
    Suppl. [II]:   1901-1911 (3 vols. in a single alphabet).
    Suppl. [III]: 1912-21.
    Suppl. [IV]: 1922-30.
    Suppl. [V]:   1931-40.
    Suppl. [VI]: 1941-50.
    Suppl. [VII]: 1951-60.
    (To clarify, the biography of a person who died between 1912 and 1921 will be found in Suppl. III.)
2)   Each supplement identifies its own contributors at the beginning of the respective volume.
3)   From Supplement III on, each Supplement has a cumulative index of lives in prior twentieth-century supplements; only birth and death dates (no page numbers) are given.

Contents and Arrangement (Corrections and Additions):

1)   Emendations arising from current research which are published in the Bulletin of the Institute of Historical Research (University of London) and are here cumulated for Bulletin volumes that appeared in 1923-63.

2) Alphabetically arranged.
3) References to the volume, page, column, and line of
   the main entry being corrected.

Review Questions:

1) John Ruskin died in 1900. In which volume of the DNB
   would you expect to find his biography? In which volume
   would you look for the biography of King George V (d.
   1936)? Of Neville Chamberlain (d. 1940)?

2) If you don't know your subject's death date, how can you
   discover it by using the DNB indexes?

3) When is it necessary to consult Corrections and Additions
   to the DNB?

4) For which of the following would you expect to find en-
   tries: Harold Pinter, John Harvard, Mahatma Gandhi,
   Henry James, Merlin, Caedmon, Joseph Lister, Benedict
   Arnold, John Millington Synge, Eugene O'Neill, Virginia
   Woolf?

5) Why was there a need for the first Supplement, which
   covers the same years as the main dictionary?

6) Which supplementary volume contains an index of all the
   twentieth-century entries?

Research Problems:

1) From the DNB entry for Oscar Wilde, can you ascertain
   for what offenses Wilde was imprisoned? Do you feel
   that the biographer's description of The Picture of Dorian
   Grey is critically clear and objective? How would you
   explain the limitations of the Wilde entry, and what does
   this suggest about the DNB as a whole?

2) Who were Benjamin Disraeli's ancestors? When did the
   D'Israelis become English citizens?

3) In what work does William Caxton speak of his parents?
   Why is he indebted to them? What is the earliest work
   printed by Caxton in England that has survived?

Notes (DNB)

1. For biographies of Americans, see the Dictionary of American Biography (S37), Who's Who in America (S38), and Who Was Who in America (S39). World-wide biographical coverage is provided by Biography Index (S40) and Essay and General Literature Index (M28); Contemporary Authors (M16) and Chambers's Biographical Dictionary (S41) provide capsule biographies. Since the DNB enters only the deceased, it may be updated with Who's Who (M15) and supplemented by Who Was Who (S36).

M15. Who's Who 1973-1974: An Annual Biographical Dictionary. New York: St. Martin's Press, 1973.

Who's Who originated in 1849 as a list of British nobility and government officials. In 1897, the "First Year of New Issue," it became the biographical dictionary it is today. Although entries for persons of rank are retained, merit is now the governing factor for eligibility. It is impossible to buy one's way into Who's Who. Reliable biographies of living British subjects make Who's Who a major tool for updating the Dictionary of National Biography.

The 1973-1974 volume of Who's Who is described below.

Contents:

1) Only living subjects. [1]
2) All fields.
3) Principally British but some entries for famous foreigners. [2]
4) Entries are for the preceding year--i. e., the 1973-1974 volume went to press November, 1972.
5) Concise biographical data: occupation, names of parents, birth date, education, awards or titles, jobs held, avocations, address, telephone, and club memberships; list of works with their dates for authors, list of films and plays with their dates for actors, etc.

Arrangement:

1) Abbreviations, pp. 7-28.
2) Obituary, pp. 29-36: lists names and death dates of those who died in the year before the volume went to press.
3) Entries for the British royal family, pp. 37-38.
4) Supplement of events occurring later than November, 1972, when the volume went to press; precedes the first page of biographies.
5) Dictionary proper, alphabetically arranged, with cross-references to other family members.

Review Questions:

1) For which of the following would you expect to find entries in the most recent volume of Who's Who: Winston Churchill, George Bernard Shaw, John Gielgud, Richard Nixon?

2) What bibliographical information is provided by Who's Who?

3) What personal information is provided? What guarantee of accuracy is given the reader?

4) In what part of the volume can you find supplementary information received too late for inclusion in its proper place?

5) What biographical reference work can Who's Who be used to update?

6) To what work are Who's Who entries transferred upon the deaths of their subjects?

Research Problems:

1) As of 1974, who was the Duke of Norfolk? When did a Howard first hold this title? What is the oldest title the present Duke holds?

2) When did F. W. Bateson, the editor of the CBEL, retire from teaching? What journal did he found? What post did he hold during World War II? What is his current address?

3) What special award did Stephen Spender receive in 1971?
    With what award was Peter Quennell honored in 1973?

Notes (Who's Who)

1. Entries are sent to each subject for yearly revision.
    Entries for the deceased are moved to Who Was Who
    (S36).

2. Note the profusion of specialized "Who's Who's," based
    upon nationality, race, profession, etc. In particular,
    see Who's Who in America (S38) and Who Was Who in
    America (S39).

M16. Etheridge, James M., ed. Contemporary Authors: A
      Bio-Bibliographical Guide to Current Authors and
      Their Works. Detroit: Gale Research, 1962--. [1]

      Contemporary Authors is international in scope, in-
cludes non-literary authors, and is issued quarterly. Thus,
its coverage is both broad and up-to-date. The incorporated
bibliographies are particularly valuable for authors not yet
well established.

Contents:

1) Currently published authors (other than vanity pub-
    lished).
2) All fields.
3) Mostly American but some prominent foreign writers.
4) Biographies verified by the subject. [2]
5) Biographical sketches subdivided into these categories:
    a. Personal--family background, education, current
        address.
    b. Career--jobs, military service, membership in
        organizations.
    c. Writing--list of works with dates. [3]
    d. Work in Progress.
    e. Sidelights--critical appraisal of major writers
        based upon judicious quotation from major critics,
        hobbies, significant statements, significant events
        in the subject's life, etc.

   f.   Biographical/Critical Sources--from newspaper and
        periodical articles and from books.
6)   Death dates of deceased authors.
7)   Obituaries: beginning with Vols. XXV-XXVIII, obituary
      citations (including lists of periodicals containing death
      notices) are incorporated into each volume and into the
      indexes.

Arrangement:

1)   Alphabetical within each volume.
2)   Cumulative index to Vols. I-XLVIII at the end of XLV-
      XLVIII.

Review Questions:

1)   For which of the following would you expect to find en-
      tries in Contemporary Authors: a writer who died before
      World War II, a writer on science, a virtually unknown
      writer, an academic literary critic?

2)   What is the nationality of most of the writers listed?

3)   Can you learn an author's death date from Contemporary
      Authors? Beginning with Vols. XXV-XXVIII, what other
      necrological information can you find?

4)   Which volume contains the most recent cumulative index?

5)   What two kinds of bibliographical information are provided
      by Contemporary Authors?

Research Problems:

1)   Where can you find death notices for the American writer
      Langston Hughes?

2)   What was Ted Hughes' first published work? To whom
      was he married? Through 1961 what prizes had he won?

3)   What was Brian Earnshaw writing in the late 1960's?
      What is the title of his science-fiction novel? Where
      can one find a review of his work?

Notes (Contemporary Authors)

1.   The first twelve volumes of the revised edition

(1967--) are now available. These volumes update
and cumulate the original series. Further volumes
of both the revised edition and continuing volumes
in the original series will appear annually.

2. The symbols + or * indicate an unverified sketch.

3. This is often not a complete bibliography; for example,
contributions to periodicals are generally not specified.

Research Problems:

1) Who is responsible for the first collected edition of Poe's letters? Of Whitman's? When did these editions appear? Has either work been superseded? Explain.

2) Cite two English language guides to philosophy published in the 1960's. How do they differ in terms of the readers to whom each work is addressed?

3) How are each of these places associated with English literature: White's, Bucklersbury, Avalon, Grub Street?

4) In what novel is the adjective "goofy" first found? (Cite date, chapter, and page.)

5) On what subject does the American professor Marvin Magalaner primarily publish? Where was he educated? To what modern literary encyclopedia has Huntington Brown, retired American professor, contributed? Where has he taught? What are his feelings about American education?

6) Name eleven Caroline dramatists. Which three seem to be the best? Whose critical opinions are you following?

7) Cite one short story and two novels in which vigilantes play a part. Which one of the authors of these works was a Californian by birth? Which of his novels won a Pulitzer Prize? Who won the Pulitzer drama award in 1940?

8) What was written in 1964 about the British playwright John Osborne? When did Osborne first achieve sufficient fame to receive critical attention? By considering the number of Osborne entries for 1970, determine whether the dramatist's reputation had grown or declined by the end of the decade. Cite the names of the books or journals in which the 1970 critical works on Osborne appeared. (Explain all title abbreviations.)

9) Approximately how many plays did Eugène Labiche have

a hand in? Give the English titles of two of his most
famous farces. What social classes does Labiche sati-
rize? What stock characters and situations does he em-
ploy? What famous German composer-poet was born
two years before Labiche? What famous Russian novelist
was born three years after Labiche?

10) What significant demographic fact led many eighteenth-
century thinkers to conclude that "America was unfit for
human beings"? How did Malthus explain population
increase in the United States?

11) What were "patent theatres"? When were the patents
finally revoked?

12) What professions are practiced by Kurt Mahler, Anna
Russell, and Alexandra Tolstoy? Who were Alexandra
Tolstoy's parents?

13) What were the first works printed and etched by William
Blake?

14) Define the following literary terms: monogatari, pluri-
signation, Secentismo, sottie.

15) In what literary sources is Minos depicted as a king associated with Zeus, ruling the dead, and married to
Pasiphae, the daughter of Helios? (Explain all abbreviations and cite exact references to the sources.)

16 How long did it take Handel to write the "Messiah"?
What is Ralph Vaughan Williams' best known piece of
incidental music to a Greek play?

CHAPTER III

BIBLIOGRAPHIES

Bibliographies of Bibliographies:

M17.   A World Bibliography of Bibliographies
M18.   Bibliographic Index

Current Bibliographies:

M19.   Specialized Bibliographies in Scholarly Journals
M20.   Checklists: Poetry Explication
M21.   The Literatures of the World in English Translation
M22.   Bibliography of American Literature
M23a. National Union Catalog: Pre-1956 Imprints
M23b. National Union Catalog: 1956--

Retrospective Bibliographies:

M24.   Short-Title Catalogue
M25.   American Bibliography

        Besterman's World Bibliography and the Bibliographic
Index are bibliographies of bibliographies; that is, they list
only bibliographies and not critical articles, biographies, etc.
Both works provide universal subject coverage.   The first
four entries under current bibliographies (M19-M22) are devoted exclusively to literature; the next, our National Union
Catalog, is in effect a bibliography of world literature, re-
stricted only by the availability of that literature in the United
States.   The retrospectively compiled STC and American Bibliography are, respectively, the foundations of the English and
American national bibliographies; for the periods covered and

and within the limits the compilers set for themselves, these listings provide the researcher with a comprehensive record of national literary output.

M17. Besterman, Theodore. A World Bibliography of Bib-
liographies and of Bibliographical Catalogues,
Calendars, Abstracts, Digests, Indexes, and the
Like. 4th ed. Revised and Greatly Enlarged
Throughout. 5 vols. Lausanne: Societas Bib-
liographica, 1965-66.

Besterman, the most complete multi-volumed list of bibliographies, is international in scope and arranged by sub- ject. It is a valuable source for retrospective book lists not subject to revision. (For example, the question, "What English translations of Classical authors were available prior to the nineteenth century?" is answered by the entry for Lewis William Brüggeman's A View of the English Editions, Translations and Illustrations of the Ancient Greek and Latin Authors, published in 1797, and found under the heading Classical Literature--Translations, English.) For bibliog- raphies of literary authors, Besterman's chief virtue lies in its convenience as a cumulated, finite work. Nevertheless, its usefulness is limited by the exclusion of all bibliographies not separately published and by the increasing obsolescence of many entries in this "really the last" edition. The stu- dent is urged, therefore, to supplement Besterman with the Bibliographic Index (M18), Nilon's Bibliography of Bibliog- raphies in American Literature (S43), and Howard-Hill's Bibliography of British Literary Biographies (S42).

Contents:

1) From the earliest bibliographies (1470) through 1963,
     with some later entries.
2) Only bibliographies separately published (i. e., with
     separate pagination)[1] and arranged according to some
     permanant principle (thus excluding publishers' and
     general libraries' catalogs); excluded also are bibliog-
     raphies in journals.
3) Both primary and secondary bibliographies.
4) Limited and privately printed editions.
5) All subjects and languages. [2]
6) Short title entries.
7) Some annotation: pagination, number of items in

each bibliography (set out in square brackets), number
of copies printed if a small edition, indication of pri-
vate printing, explanation of ambiguous or inaccurate
titles, clarification of works in series, etc.

Arrangement:

1) A list of subject headings for subjects classified by
   countries, Vol. I, Introduction, pp. 41-42.
2) A list of subheadings under a country classified by
   subjects, Vol. I, Introduction, pp. 43-44.
3) Bibliography proper: arranged alphabetically by subject; subject headings usually quite broad.
4) Within the subject heading or subheading, chronologically by date of publication.
5) Extensive cross-references.
6) Index: Vol. V;[4] includes in one alphabet authors, editors, translators, titles of anonymous and serial bibliographies, libraries, archives, and patents.

Review Questions:

1) Is Besterman limited to bibliographies of literary subjects?

2) For which of the following would you expect to find entries:
   a. a bibliography appended to a dissertation on Keats?
   b. a bibliographical pamphlet on theatrical and literary
      British journals, published as part of a series?
   c. a calendar (list of manuscripts) of the Byron holdings
      in the University of Texas library?
   d. a separately published bibliography on Tennyson that
      appeared in 1966?
   e. a French language bibliography of ancient and modern
      authors, published in 1704?
   f. a bibliography of Jane Austen's letters? A critical
      bibliography of Jane Austen?

3) How can you determine the extent of the bibliographies
   entered?

4) What indication of availability does Besterman provide?

5) What principles of arrangement does Besterman follow
   for subject entries? Within the subject heading?

6) Would you find Goethe cited in the Index? Satan?
   Besterman?

Research Problems:

1) What separately published bibliography was compiled by
   the critic, poet, and novelist Allen Tate? For what
   bibliography did Tate serve as adviser?

2) Cite a twentieth-century catalog of the Robin Hood holdings of the public libraries in Nottingham. How many
   works are entered? Cite a more recent general bibliography of Robin Hood. How extensive is this work?

3) Cite a bibliography of English Bibles printed between
   1526 and 1776. Where can one find copies of the original editions of this bibliography containing manuscript
   notes and additions?

Notes (Besterman)

1. Bibliographies appended to book-length critical studies
   or to critical studies in periodicals are excluded.

2. Works, in, though not on, Oriental languages are excluded. Works in Eastern European languages are
   minimally represented.

3. London and Paris are understood as the places of publication for English and French works, respectively,
   if no other place is cited.

4. Note that pagination is continuous through all five volumes.

M18. Bibliographic Index: A Cumulative Bibliography of
      Bibliographies. New York: H. W. Wilson,
      1938--.

   BI is a universal subject listing of bibliographies published separately and, unlike Besterman (M17), of bibliographies included in books and in periodical articles. Currently cumulated annually, [1] BI both supplements and updates

Besterman. Its major value for students of literature is as
a current index to bibliographies of British, American, and
Western European authors. [2]   Since most literary authors
are treated as subjects, BI's subject classification presents
little difficulty.

Contents:

1)   Bibliographies: those published separately.
2)   Bibliographies: those appearing as parts of books,
     pamphlets, and periodicals.
3)   Chiefly English, French, Italian, German, and Spanish
     language works indexed.
4)   With regard to literary subjects, generally limited to
     author (rather than title) entries; only anonymous works
     receive separate citations.
5)   Literary genres and movements found under the ap-
     propriate subject headings.
6)   Only extensive bibliographies cited: fifty or more
     titles.
7)   Unannotated. [3]
8)   Coverage: generally current, but some entries may
     escape the editors for a year or more, as is the
     case with almost all universal reference works.

Arrangement:

1)   Keys to periodical and general abbreviations.
2)   Index proper: broad subject headings and subject sub-
     divisions arranged alphabetically. [4]
3)   Within the subject heading, bibliographies listed alpha-
     betically by author. [5]
4)   Within the literary author heading, first primary ("by"),
     then secondary ("about") bibliographies.
5)   Cross-references:
     a.   from pseudonyms to entry name.
     b.   from subjects to related topics, e.g., "Comedy,
          See also Tragicomedy." [6]

Review Questions:

1)   Is the BI limited to bibliographies on English and Ameri-
     can literature?

2)   Are the listed bibliographies annotated by the editors of
     BI?

3) To locate a book-length study, in English, of a major literary figure--a study containing an extensive, annotated bibliography--would BI or the MLA International Bibliography be the more useful tool? Why?

4) For which of the following might you expect to find entries:
   a. a bibliographical treatment of exorcism, published in a popular, general interest magazine?
   b. bibliographies on the anonymous Song of Roland?
   c. a scholarly bibliography in a pamphlet on Bertolt Brecht?
   d. a bibliography on romanticism in art, published in a periodical?
   e. a bibliographic essay written in French about T. S. Eliot?

Research Problems:

1) Find a bibliography of works about the American poet, critic, and scholar John Berryman, published late in the 1960's. Cite full publishing information. Is this work devoted exclusively to bibliography, or is the bibliography only a small part of the work? When was Berryman born?

2) Cite a book published in 1972 that contains a bibliography of works dealing with Jews in literature. Under what Bibliographic Index subject heading did you find this title? Under what other headings would you be likely to find bibliographies on this subject?

3) Cite a 1951 literary study with bibliography of the self-proclaimed descendant and namesake of Lord Byron, who styled himself Major Byron. How extensive is the work's bibliography? Is it annotated?

Notes (BI)

1. Permanent volumes containing bibliographies published between 1937 and 1968 are cumulated in periods varying between two and six years.

2. Also see Howard-Hill's Bibliography of British Literary Bibliographies (S42) and Nilon's Bibliography of Bibliographies in American Literature (S43).

3. But annotation within the bibliography listed is indicated
    by the abbreviation "annot." Among other features,
    such annotation makes Bibliographic Index more useful
    as a guide to bibliographies than the MLA International
    Bibliography, since the latter does not indicate annota-
    tion.

4. Subdivision headings, which follow Library of Congress
    classifications, are more specific than those in Bester-
    man.

5. Prior to 1955, bibliographies were listed alphabetically
    by title.

6. References to related subjects and to subheadings must
    be carefully examined. See the Prefatory Note at
    the front of each volume for sample entries interpret-
    ing Bibliographic Index entry style.

M19. Specialized Bibliographies in Scholarly Journals

Many scholarly journals regularly include a bibliography of current works on a particular subject, often the
subject to which the journal is devoted. The advantages of
such specialized bibliographies over the MLA International
Bibliography (M7) are these:

1) the latter often fails to meet its publication deadline
    (e.g., the 1971 issue did not appear until June, 1973),
    whereas the specialized scholarly journals are up-to-
    date.
2) some specialized journals publish bibliographies as
    often as biannually or quarterly.
3) some publish annotated bibliographies.
4) some specialized serial bibliographies (i.e., bibliog-
    raphies appearing within journals) may be more com-
    prehensive than the MLA listings; others are evalua-
    tive and selective, listing only important titles pub-
    lished that year.
5) serial bibliographies covering a period of years are
    often collected and published in book form for the re-
    searcher's convenience.

Below are a number of scholarly journals, the titles of their
bibliographies, and relevant information.

M19a.   American Literature: "Articles on American Litera-
        ture Appearing in Current Periodicals" [1929--]. [1]
        Appears quarterly. Minimally annotated check-
        list. [2] Classified by period. Followed by Key to
        Abbreviations. All bibliography items from 1929
        through 1967 are included in Lewis Leary's Arti-
        cles on American Literature 1900-1950 (S49a) and
        its supplement, Articles on American Literature
        1950-1967 (S49b).

M19b.   American Quarterly: "Articles in American Studies"
        [1954--]. Selective interdisciplinary bibliography
        of scholarly articles in all fields relating to Amer-
        ican culture. Appears annually. Annotated. Cur-
        rently subdivided by subject: Art and Architec-
        ture, Education, Literature, Religion, etc.

M19c.   Studies in English Literature 1500-1900: "Recent
        Studies in English Renaissance" [1961--, winter
        issues]; "Recent Studies in Elizabethan and
        Jacobean Drama" [1961--, spring issues]. An-
        nual evaluative bibliographical essays surveying
        the year's scholarship on English Renaissance
        subjects.

M19d.   Shakespeare Quarterly: "An Annotated World Bibliog-
        raphy" [1949--]. Appears annually. Classified
        (see Arrangement of Contents) and comprehensive;
        records all books, dissertations, articles, and re-
        views of books and theatrical productions directly
        related to Shakespeare. Brief descriptions of
        contents or statements of theme for all articles
        and some books.

M19e.   Shakespeare Survey: "The Year's Contributions to
        Shakespearian Study" [1948--]. Annual evaluative
        bibliographic essays. Division into three cata-
        gories: Critical Studies; Shakespeare's Life,
        Times, and Stage; Textual Studies.

M19f.   Philological Quarterly: "The Eighteenth Century: A
        Current Bibliography incorporating English Litera-
        ture 1660-1800" [1926--]. Appears annually.
        Currently a selective, partially annotated[3] bibliog-
        raphy of books, articles, and reviews on eight-
        eenth-century England, America, and continental
        Europe. Classified (see Contents) and interdis-
        ciplinary; catagories include such extra-literary

areas as social and economic studies. Index of
authors (primary and secondary), editors, and reviewers at end. Bibliographies for 1925-1970 are
collected in English Literature, 1660-1800: A
Bibliography of Modern Studies Founded by Ronald
S. Crane (Princeton: Princeton University Press,
1950--).[4] Six volumes to date; supplementary
volumes will be issued every several years.

M19g.   English Language Notes: "The Romantic Movement:
A Selective and Critical Bibliography" [1965--].[5]
Appears annually. A selective, classified bibliography of romanticism in England and sometimes on the
continent. Major division by nationality. Descriptive, sometimes critical, annotation of books, articles, and reviews. Locates further critical reviews.

M19h.   Victorian Studies: "Victorian Bibliography" [1958--].[6]
Appears annually. Partially annotated[7] bibliography
of books, dissertations, articles, and reviews.
Classified: I. Bibliographical Material; II. Economic, Political, Religious, and Social Environ-
ment; III. Movements of Ideas and Literary
Forms; IV. Individual Authors. Bibliographies
for 1932-64 are collected in Bibliographies of Studies in Victorian Literature, 3 vols. (Urbana, Ill.:
University of Illinois Press, 1945-67).

M19i.   Twentieth-Century Literature: "Current Bibliography
[of Twentieth-Century Literature]" [1954--]. Appears quarterly. Bibliography of current critical articles in American and foreign periodicals on modern
world literature. Annotated. Arranged alphabetically by primary author with general subjects alphabetically interspersed. For an expanded cumulation, see
David E. Pownall, Articles on Twentieth Century Literature: An Annotated Bibliography 1954 to 1970
(New York: Kraus-Thomson, 1974--). Four volumes
(A-L) to date.

Review Questions:

1)   In what ways are specialized journal bibliographies unlike
the MLA International Bibliography?

2)   Which journals carry bibliographies of American literature?

3)   Where can one find annual evaluative surveys of criticisr

dealing with American literature?

4) Which two journal bibliographies are published quarterly?

5) Which journals contain an annual bibliography of Renais-
    sance studies? Of Shakespeare? Of Victorian literature?

6) In which journal can you find a bibliography of the Res-
    toration and eighteenth century? Where are these bibli-
    ographies collected?

7) Which other annual bibliographies have been collected
    and printed in book form?

Research Problems:

1) Using a specialized serial bibliography, find a précis of
    Elmo Howell's "Eudora Welty's Comedy of Manners"
    (Autumn 1970).

2) Using a specialized serial bibliography, discover the
    thesis of J. L. Kendall's "A Neglected Theme in Ten-
    nyson's In Memoriam" (1961). Give full publication data
    for this article.

3) Using an annual bibliographic essay, note the main in-
    terests of English Renaissance students in 1970.

Notes (Spec. Biblio.)

1. Bracketed dates refer to the year in which bibliographical
    coverage begins; this date may not necessarily coincide
    with the founding of the periodical.

2. For full annotation, see American Literary Scholarship
    (S48).

3. Evaluative bibliographical essays on significant scholar-
    ship dealing with English literature of the Restoration
    and eighteenth century can be found in the summer issues
    of Studies in English Literature 1500-1900 (M19c).

4. This work is sometimes referred to as "Landa" after
    Louis A. Landa, one of its editors and author of the
    Foreword to the first volume.

5. During 1937-49, "The Romantic Movement" appeared

in ELH: A Journal of English Literary History, during 1950-64 in Philological Quarterly.

6. During 1933-57, "Victorian Bibliography" appeared annually in Modern Philology.

7. Evaluative bibliographical essays on significant scholarship dealing with English literature of the nineteenth
century can be found in the autumn issues of Studies
in English Literature 1500-1900 (M19c).

M20. Checklists

Kuntz, Joseph M. Poetry Explication: A Checklist
of Interpretation Since 1925 of British and American Poems Past and Present. Rev. ed. Denver:
Alan Swallow, 1962.

Kuntz's Poetry Explication is one example of a checklist: the simplest and shortest form of a bibliography. Often selective rather than comprehensive, and usually unannotated, a checklist may be devoted to a single work, e.g.,
Samuel A. Tannenbaum, Shakespeare's "King Lear": A Concise Bibliography (New York: Samuel A. Tannenbaum, 1940);
to a single author, listing works by and/or about him, e.g.,
The Merrill Checklist of Nathaniel Hawthorne, comp. C. E.
Frazer Clark, Jr. (Columbus, Ohio: Charles E. Merrill,
1970); or to a broad subject, e.g., Tudor and Stuart Drama,
comp. Irving Ribner (New York: Appleton, 1966). [1]
Kuntz's Poetry Explication is described below.

Contents:

1) Generally treats poems of not more than 500 lines.
2) Recognized poets.
3) Only explicatory criticisms published between 1925
and 1959. [2]
4) Only criticisms from easily available books and periodicals; excludes criticism from books devoted to
single authors.

Arrangement:

1) Alphabetical by author; within the author entry, alphabetical by title.

2)   Main Sources Consulted at end.

Review Questions:

1)   How does a checklist differ from such standard bibliographies as the New CBEL or the LHUS: Bibliography?

2)   What would you suppose is the main advantage of a checklist?

3)   What kinds of criticism are not included in Poetry Explication?

4)   What kinds of poets and poems are not treated?

Research Problems:

1)   On which of Wordsworth's poems has F. R. Leavis written explicatory criticism?

2)   Cite two explicatory criticisms by John Crowe Ransom of
Yeats' "Sailing to Byzantium."

3)   Cite an explicatory criticism of the anonymous medieval
poem, "Nutbrowne Mayde." (Give full publication information for the source you cite.)

Notes (Checklists)

1.   Some particularly useful checklists are Modern Drama
(S63), The English Novel 1578-1956 (S46), The Ameri-
can Novel 1789-1959 (S51), The Continental Novel
(S60), Short Fiction Criticism (S61), Twentieth-Cen-
tury Short Story Explication (S62), and Greek and
Roman Authors: A Checklist of Criticism (M11, n. 4).

2.   For more recent criticism, see the checklists of expli-
cations published annually in The Explicator, a journal
of short criticisms.

M21.   The Literatures of the World in English Translation:
A Bibliography. New York: Frederick Ungar,
1967--.

Three volumes of a projected five volumes have been
published as of 1970:

Vol. I: The Greek and Latin Literatures.   Ed. George
    B. Parks and Ruth Z. Temple. New York: Fred-
    erick Ungar, 1968.
Vol. II: The Slavic Literatures.   Comp. Richard C.
    Lewanski.   The New York Public Library and
    Frederick Ungar, 1967.
Vol. III: The Romance Literature.   Ed. George B.
    Parks and Ruth Z. Temple. 2 parts. New York:
    Frederick Ungar, 1970.
Vol. IV (The Celtic, Germanic and Other Literatures
    of Europe) and Vol. V (The Literatures of Asia
    and Africa) are in preparation.

This series is not only a bibliography of foreign literary works in translation but also a guide to the non-English literatures.   That is, the background sections on general literature, on particular national literatures, and on
literary periods are as valuable as the author listings. More-
over, in all but the Slavic volume, literature is interpreted
in its widest sense as writings in the humanities. Note, too,
that The Literatures of the World in English Translation is
to some degree evaluative. The most important translations
are indicated by an asterisk. Generally it is these works
that the student will want to use or investigate.
    Volume I, The Greek and Latin Literatures, is de-
scribed below in detail. Volumes II and III are described
only with regard to their notable differences from Volume I.

Vol. I: The Greek and Latin Literatures:

Contents:

1)   Imaginative literature; literary history and criticism;
    the greater works of history, philosophy, theology,
    law, and science. [1] Excluded are specialized works
    in science and the humanities, textbooks, collections
    of documents, children's books, and sub-literature.
2)   All translations from the earliest to 1965. [2] However,
    "for a few frequently retranslated authors, such as
    Dante, we abridge our list to include the more im-
    portant and more recent translations, making cross-
    reference to other special bibliographies" (The Plan
    of the Book).
3)   Some annotation: note that an asterisk designates an
    especially important translation.

4) Prefatory annotated bibliography of general literature: collective bibliographies of literature in translation, collective histories of literature, collections of translations from more than one literature, and books on the history and theory of translation.

5) Background chapters: bibliographies of cultural and historical studies of Greek and Roman literature, including classical, Christian, Byzantine, and modern writing.

6) Individual authors.

Arrangement:

1) Table of Contents, pp. ix-x.
2) Abbreviations, pp. xvii-xix.
3) Generally chronological order; after the first two background chapters ("General Reference" and "Greek and Roman Literature"), Greek Literature precedes Latin.
4) Within conventional chronological periods, individual authors are listed alphabetically. [3]
5) Within the author entry, works are listed alphabetically by title of the English translation. (For prolific authors, first collected, then selected, and then individual works are cited.)
6) Successive translations of a given work are listed chronologically. [4]
7) Index of translated authors, anonymous works, and anthologies, pp. 431-42.

Contents and Arrangement (Vol. II: The Slavic Literatures):

1) Prefatory chapter corresponding to (4) above lists only general anthologies, i.e., comprehensive works with translations from more than one language.
2) Limited to belles lettres.
3) Coverage through 1960.
4) Alphabetical arrangement by language.
5) Within the language:
   a. a list of anthologies (of several authors) with a description of their contents, each anthology being numbered for cross-reference;[5] and
   b. a list of individual authors arranged alphabetically; collected works precede individual works. [6]
6) No division into chronological periods; authors' birth and death dates not provided
7) Anonymous Works section at the end of each particular Slavic Literature.

8)   Index of translated authors and individual titles, pp.
      447-618.
      Index of Anthologies and Compilers, pp. 621-
      30.

Contents and Arrangement (Vol. III: The Romance Literatures):

1)   Coverage through 1968.
2)   In two parts, each part bound separately:
      Part 1: Catalan, Italian, Portuguese, Brazilian,
               Provençal, Rumanian, Spanish, Spanish Amer-
               ican (in this last category, a heading for co-
               lonial literature precedes the alphabetical list
               of individual countries).
      Part 2: Literature of France and French literature of
               other countries (Belgium, Switzerland, Can-
               ada, Louisiana, West Indies, Africa).

Review Questions, Vols. I-III:

1)   For which of these works would you expect to find a list-
      ing of translations: Zorba the Greek, the Latin writings
      of the mystic Emmanuel Swedenborg, Marx's Das Kapital,
      Doctor Zhivago, the stories of Sholom Aleichem, Edith
      Piaf's Autobiography, the Marquis de Sade's Justine,
      Garcia Lorca's Blood Wedding?

2)   Would you expect to find a complete listing of translations
      of Plato's The Republic? Of Virgil's Aeneid? Of Dio-
      dorus of Sicily's History?

3)   How can perusing The Literatures of the World in Eng-
      lish Translation help you to learn about the taste of
      various eras?

4)   Explain this entry under Chekhov:
           Peasants (tr C Garnett)
              In: Yarmolinsky (see Rus 154).

Research Problems:

1)   Which two of Ugo Betti's plays are most frequently re-
      printed in English anthologies?

2)   Name Pablo Picasso's French play. Who translated it
      into English? Cite full publishing information.

3) List the English translations of Henry VIII's attack on Luther, written in Latin.

Notes (Lit. World)

1. Remember that this is not merely a bibliography of classical literature. Translations of twentieth-century Greek literature are listed; and in the Addenda (p. 429), you will find a neo-Latin work by a Roman Catholic priest born in 1880.

2. Continuing annual bibliographies of translations can be found in the Index Translationum (S77) and the Yearbook of Comparative and General Literature (S58).

3. The compiler also notes the authors' birth and death dates and whether a work is in verse or prose.

4. "Translations of Latin works of English authors are not included if the translation was published during the author's lifetime..." (p. 341).

5. "For example; under Brezina:
        The Anniversary
            In: Ginsberg (see Czech 10)
    refers to the story The Anniversary which appeared in the anthology compiled by Roderick A. Ginsberg, item 10 in the Czech Literature Anthologies section..." (Preface).

6. "Titles in an author's collected works are not included in the section of separate Individual Titles, but all versions of a title can be located through the index" (Preface).

M22. Blanck, Jacob, comp. Bibliography of American Literature. New Haven: Yale University Press, 1955--. (Six volumes, the last in 1973, have appeared to date--Henry Adams to Thomas William Parsons.)

The BAL is the definitive American descriptive bibliography. That is, Blanck not only provides standard bibliographical data but also notes the physical characteristics of the earliest editions and published revisions of his entries. Though selective, Blanck lists more authors than does the LHUS: Bibliography (M6). The latter work, however, is the standard source for important secondary bibliographies of authors and for background to American literature.

Contents:

1) Selected authors significant in the history of American literature from the Revolution on, excluding those who died after 1930 and those who primarily wrote juvenilia.
2) All first editions of the author's works.
3) Any book or pamphlet, etc. (excluding periodical or newspaper publications) containing the first appearance of any prose (except letters) by the author.
4) Variant issues or states of the first edition. [1]
5) Illustrations, maps, binding.
6) European editions in English that preceded the American edition.
7) Reprints that might be confused with first editions or with editions containing important textual changes.
8) Sheet music.
9) Some off-[literary] subject books.
10) List of bibliographical, biographical, and critical works about the author ("Reference").
11) Locates works examined, although not a census. [2]

Arrangement:

1) Location symbols at front of each volume.
2) Alphabetical by author.
3) Within the author entry, chronological by date of publication.
4) List of secondary sources at end of each author entry.
5) Initials, Pseudonymns, and Anonyms at end of each volume.

Review Questions:

1) What outstanding feature of the BAL distinguishes it from other general bibliographies of American literature?

2) Would you expect to find an entry for William Faulkner? For the colonial poetess Anne Bradstreet? For Ralph Waldo Emerson?

3) Does the BAL note the first publication of a work that originally appeared in an anthology? In a magazine?

4) Would you find entries citing European editions of American works?

5) Can the BAL be used for finding secondary source material?

Research Problems:

1) When was Crane's Maggie: A Girl of the Streets originally published? What pseudonym did Crane use? When was the revised edition of Maggie published? Note two ways in which, by examining the title-pages with regard to publisher's name and publication date, the first edition of Maggie can be distinguished from the revised edition.

2) What was William Dean Howells' first publication? When, where, and in what format was it published? At what library can it be seen?

3) List the complete literary works (with dates) of William Hill Brown, considered the first American novelist. Mention one modern bio-bibliographical study of Brown.

Notes (BAL)

1. An issue consists of copies of a printing altered after initial publication. A state consists of those copies altered prior to publication or sale. See Blanck's Preface for a discussion of these terms and for an explanation of his entry form. Incidentally, the Preface to the BAL can seve as a pleasant capsule introduction to descriptive bibliography.

2. A literary census is a comprehensive listing, locating all examples of a particular class. See, for example, The National Union Catalog of Manuscript Collections Based on Reports from American Repositories of Manuscripts (Ann Arbor, Michigan: J. W. Edwards, 1951-61--) and Seymour de Ricci, Census of Medieval and Renaissance Manuscripts in the United States and Canada, 3 vols. (1934-40; rpt. New York: Kraus, 1961).
    Blanck has attempted personally to examine

all the works he enters in order to minimize "ghosts."
When he has been unable to do so, he cites his
source.

M23a.   The National Union Catalog. Pre-1956 Imprints:
        A Cumulative Author List Representing Library
        of Congress Printed Cards and Titles Reported
        by Other American Libraries. London: Mansell,
        1968--. (To date, 364 of a projected 610 vols.)

M23b.   The National Union Catalog: A Cumulative Author
        List Representing Library of Congress Printed
        Cards and Titles Reported by Other American
        Libraries. Washington: Library of Congress,
        1956--. (This is the ongoing continuation of our
        national union catalog, appearing monthly with
        quarterly, annual, and quinquennial cumulations,
        and now up to its 1968-72 cumulation.)

        A national union catalog is a listing of publications
held by a nation's major library (in America, the Library
of Congress)[1] and by important research libraries throughout
that country. Because of its comprehensiveness, the accuracy of its entries, and the extensive descriptions of the
works entered, our national union catalog is a valuable research tool for verification of bibliographical data and for
locating hard-to-find publications.
        The current U.S. national catalog is an outgrowth of
the old "LC Catalog," basically an author list of publications
held by the Library of Congress up through 1942.[2] Although
supplements to the "LC Catalog" were issued regularly,[3] it
was not until 1956 that those books not in the Library of
Congress collection but held by other American libraries
were also listed and located. The source of difficulty for
the novice researcher is that the conversion of the "LC Catalog" into a union catalog will not be completed for another
five years. At that time one will be able to trace any work
through the two catalogs described below: Pre-1956 Imprints
and the ongoing NUC [1956--]. Presently, however, until
Pre-1956 Imprints is completed, one may have to work with
a number of partial and interim sets. These include 1) the
"LC Catalog" (S53); 2) either its supplements or Gale Research's master cumulation for 1942-1962 (S54), which does
not become a union catalog until 1956; and 3) The National
Union Catalog: 1952-1955 Imprints: An Author List Repre-

senting Library of Congress Printed Cards and Titles Reported by Other American Libraries, 30 vols. (Ann Arbor: J. W. Edwards, 1961)--this last being a retrospective NUC listing.

Consider two research problems, the first simple, the second more demanding. To verify the title of a work on Falstaff by Hermann Kurz (the date of which is unknown to you), you would first check Pre-1956 Imprints, complete through "K"; if not found there, you would search the NUC cumulations for 1956 on. But to verify bibliographical data on a reprinted volume of carols edited by Thomas Wright (date of reprinting unknown), you would have to use the accessory sets, since Pre-1956 Imprints will not reach "W" until the late 1970's. Thus you would first check the old "LC Catalog"; if not found, the Gale cumulation through 1962 (or the original LC Supplements); and, if still not found, the ongoing NUC cumulations. (It should be mentioned that not all reprints are included in Pre-1956 Imprints or in the ongoing NUC; most frequently omitted are reprints of works whose originals have been catalogued.) One case cannot be found in any LC set: a work held by a library other than the Library of Congress, whose author's name falls in the last part of the alphabet and which was not catalogued until after 1952.

Contents (Pre-1956 Imprints):

1) Selected entries from the collections of major research libraries in the U.S. and Canada (the most important of course, being the Library of Congress which holds the copyright privilege).

2) Rare items in other collections. [4]

3) Only works printed or manuscripts written before 1956. (Some 10,000,000 entries are anticipated.)

4) Works in all languages.

5) Books, pamphlets, maps, atlases, and music; some periodicals and other serials. [5]

6) Extensive bibliographical data: author and his dates, full title, edition, [6] place and date of publication, pagination, special features (e.g., maps, bibliography), historical notes where relevant, LC subject classification, LC number, and copyright number. The contents of composite works and periodicals are often analyzed at length.

7) Locations: based upon some seven hundred North American libraries; if no locations are designated, it may be assumed that the work is available at the Library of Congress.

Arrangement:

1) Detailed instructions for use, Vol. I, pp. xi-xix.
2) Alphabetical by author;[7] under the author listing, usually alphabetical by title. Some title entries where no author is indicated.
3) Anonymous works entered under the supplied authors with cross-references to title entries. [8]
4) Extensive added entries for co-authors, editors, translators, etc. as well as cross-references.
5) Locating symbols on endpapers of each volume.

Below are described notable dissimilarities between Pre-1956 Imprints and the NUC [1956--].

Contents and Arrangement (NUC, 1956--)

1) Works for which cards have been printed from 1956 on, regardless of the dates of the publications themselves.
2) Register of Additional Locations: constituted by the last volumes of each NUC quinquennial cumulation.
3) Explanation of entry form and locating symbols only at the front of the first volume of each cumulation.

Review Questions:

1) What is a national union catalog? How is it useful to students of literature?

2) When was the "LC Catalog" first converted into a national union catalog? For what three-year period has it been retrospectively converted? (That is, cite a set not in progress but complete.)

3) To what do the dates used in the LC's or NUC's titles refer?

4) Is every book in every major library in the U.S. and Canada entered in Pre-1956 Imprints and its NUC continuation?

5) What publications other than books are entered?

6) Are only English language works entered?

7) If no location symbols appear for an entry, is the work widely available?

8)   Are main entries arranged by author, title, or subject?

9)   Is a subject listing of the LC entries available?

10) Describe the extent of the bibliographical data you would
     expect to find for Pre-1956 Imprints or NUC main en-
     tries published in the twentieth century.

11) For which of the following would you expect to find en-
     tries in Pre-1956 Imprints:
     a.   a nineteenth-century edition of Defoe's Robinson
          Crusoe acquired by the Library of Congress shortly
          after its publication?
     b.   a first edition of Hemingway's For Whom the Bell
          Tolls (1940)?
     c.   a first edition of a sixteenth-century English Bible
          acquired by the Huntington Library prior to 1956,
          but not held by the Library of Congress?
     d.   a first edition of Nathanael West's Miss Lonely-
          hearts (1933)?

12) For which of the following would you expect to find en-
     tries in the NUC [1956--]:
     a.   John Fowles' The French Lieutenant's Woman (1969)?
     b.   a 1963 reprint of an English translation of Dostoyev-
          sky's Notes from Underground?
     c.   an important post-1956 anthology of poetry in Japa-
          nese?
     d.   a University of Minnesota pamphlet by Robert E.
          Spiller on James Fenimore Cooper (1965)?

13) Is the British Museum Catalogue a national union cata-
     log?

Research Problems:

1)   Cite the full title, author, and imprint of Charles Kings-
     ley's The Tutor's Story. Which American library holds
     the original British edition?

2)   In 1924, what important avant-garde press reprinted
     T. S. Eliot's essay on Andrew Marvell? Which Ameri-
     can libraries hold copies of this reprinting? Where was
     the essay originally published? Cite issue and page ref-
     erence.

3)   Using the NUC, prepare a list of foreign translations

published in the 1960's of Gregory Corso's writings.
What specific works does each volume of translation contain? Locate copies of these translations in American
libraries.

Notes (NUC)

1. Great Britain's national library is the British Museum.
    The British Museum General Catalogue (S52) is, how-
    ever, just that and not a union catalog.

2. Dates used in the Library of Congress' or National Union
    Catalog's titles refer to the year in which library
    cards were printed for the books entered, not to when
    those books were published (although, especially after
    1942, the year of card printing and the year of publi-
    cation may often coincide). Thus, if in 1958 the Li-
    brary of Congress--or some other major North Ameri-
    can library--received a book printed in 1768, that book
    will appear in the 1958 NUC cumulation.

3. Of these Supplements, the first--1942-1947--is still use-
    ful for its title approach to some 26,000 anonymous
    and pseudonymous titles. (These works are filed un-
    der both attributed author and title, but in each case
    the name of the supplied author is crossed out though
    still legible.) Also see the Dictionary of Anonymous
    and Pseudonymous Literature (S1), the British Museum
    General Catalogue (S52), Nineteenth-Century Reader's
    Guide (S75), The Wellesley Index (S76), and those
    works mentioned under M24 and M25 that constitute
    the British and American national bibliographies.

4. For further coverage, see Subject Collections: A Guide
    to Special Book Collections and Subject Emphases as
    Reported by University, College, Public, and Special
    Libraries in the United States and Canada, comp. Lee
    Ash and Dennis Lorenz, 3rd ed., rev. and enl. (New
    York and London: R. R. Bowker, 1967).

5. More comprehensive serial coverage can be found in the
    Union List of Serials (S79); in New Serial Titles (S79,
    passim); and in Ulrich's International Periodicals Di-
    rectory (M31); also see the Introduction to Vol. I of
    Pre-1956 Imprints, p. xi.
        Note that phonorecords, motion pictures, and

filmstrips, books in Braille, and most M. A. theses
are excluded; however, the Library of Congress pre-
pares ongoing union catalogs of music and phonorec-
ords and of motion pictures and filmstrips. Also
available are an NUC of Manuscript Collections and a
National Register of Microform Masters.

6. Included are separate entries for different editions and
    issues.

7. For a subject listing, see The LC Catalog--Books:
    Subjects (S55).

8. Note that the NUC is an important source of attributions.

M24. Pollard, A. W., and G. R. Redgrave. A Short-Title
      Catalogue of Books Printed in England, Scotland,
      and Ireland and of English Books Printed Abroad
      1475-1640. London: The Bibliographical Society,
      1926.

        Pollard and Redgrave's bibliography is drawn from
the register of the Stationers' (printers') Company, incorporated in 1557. According to the Company's regulations, each
member had to enter in the register the names of all books
he wished to print. Since, for the most part, only members
of the Stationers' Company were allowed to print books, the
register facilitated governmental censorship of the press.
        Today, Pollard and Redgrave's Short-[abridged] Title
Catalogue of the register facilitates literary scholarship by
providing a systematic listing of extant early English publications. [1] As such, the STC is a vital part of the British national bibliography, i. e., a collection of bibliographies offer-
ing a complete record of the publications printed in a country
(or concerning that country) from the beginning of printing
to the present time.

Contents:

    1) Books in all languages printed between 1475 and 1640
        in the British Isles. [2]
    2) All books in English wherever printed. [3]
    3) Abridged or "short" titles of books entered.
    4) Extensive bibliographical information: generally in-
        cludes names of translators, editors, subjects of
        bibliographies, persons attacked, as well as a

description of the book's format (folio, octavo, etc.),
the printer's name, place of publication, and year of
entry. [4]

5) Variant editions and issues noted.

6) Locates some copies in British Isles and U.S.A. but
not a complete census. [5]

Arrangement:

1) Explanation of abbreviations of libraries and owners,
pp. xv-xvi.

2) Alphabetical arrangement by author's name.

3) Anonymous works: listed under author's name if author has been identified; otherwise, listed under the
first proper name in the title or, if there is no proper
name, under the first substantive.

4) Entry numbers for all main entries; entry numbers
for some variant editions and issues.

5) STC entry numbers at top of page; page numbers at
bottom of page in parenthesis.

6) Cross-references: sometimes by entry number only,
sometimes by heading, or by both.

Review Questions:

1) What is the Stationers' Register?

2) For which of the following would you expect to find entries: Holinshed's Chronicles (a source for many of
Shakespeare's plays); a regulation concerning tithing in
London; Giovanni Paoli Lomazzo's work on painting, published in English translation at the end of the sixteenth
century; the English Jesuit John Rastell's tracts against
the Church of England, published in Antwerp in the mid-
sixteenth century?

3) What sort of bibliographical information does the STC
provide? If no place of publication is entered, where
was the work published?

4) What is the STC's main principle of arrangement?

5) How can the STC be helpful to the student who has no
access to libraries that hold original editions?

Research Problems:

1) How many separate editions of Love's Labour's Lost

appeared during Shakespeare's lifetime (1564-1616)?
Under what cover title did this edition appear? Who
printed it? Where can the original volume be seen?

2) When and by whom were these anonymous ballads first
printed: "This maide would give tenne shillings for a
kisse" and "Fond love why dost thou dally: or the passion-
ate lovers ditty"? When was the following anonymous work
entered in the Stationers' register, and where can an original copy be seen: "The forme and shape of a monstrous
child borne at Maydstone"? (See Maidstone.)

3) What work of Jacques Cartier's was published in England
in the sixteenth century? Cite the translator, printer,
year, and place of publication; describe the format of the
book. What British and American libraries and collectors hold original copies?

Notes (STC)

1. The user should be warned, however, that hundreds of
"ghosts" (non-existent books) have been discovered in
the STC, that as many as ten percent of extant books
and twenty percent of extant editions and variant issues may have escaped the compilers' net, and that
entries are not consistently thorough. As Pollard and
Redgrave point out, the STC "is a dangerous work for
anyone to handle lazily, that is, without verification"
(Preface). The user will find additions and corrections in the News Sheet of the Bibliographical Society
of the University of Virginia.

 Further additions to the STC include Paul G.
Morrison, Index of Printers, Publishers, and Booksellers [in Pollard and Redgrave] (Charlottesville, Va.:
Bibliographical Society of the University of Virginia,
1961); William Warner Bishop, A Checklist of American Copies of "Short-Title Catalogue" Books, 2nd ed.
(Ann Arbor: University of Michigan Press, 1950);
and David Ramage, A Finding-List of English Books
to 1640 in Libraries in the British Isles (Durham:
Council of Durham Colleges, 1958).

2. The British national bibliography can be constructed from
the following works:
Arber, Edward. A Transcript of Registers of the
 Company of Stationers of London, 1554-1640 A.D.
 5 vols. 1875-94; rpt. New York: Peter Smith,

1950. (Largely superseded by the STC; does,
however, include nonextant books.)

Wing, Donald. Short-Title Catalogue of Books Printed
in England, Scotland, Ireland, Wales, and British
America and of English Books Printed in Other
Countries 1641-1700. (S64).

[Eyre, G. E. B.] A Transcript of the Registers of the
Worshipful Company of Stationers from 1640-1708
A. D. 3 vols. 1913-14; rpt. New York: Peter
Smith, 1950.

Arber, Edward. The Term Catalogues, 1668-1709
A. D. , with a Number for the Easter Term 1711
A. D.: A Contemporary Bibliography of English
Literature in the Reigns of Charles II, James II,
William and Mary, and Anne. 3 vols. 1903-06;
rpt. New York: Johnson Reprint Corp., 1965.
(A contemporary list edited from London book-
sellers' quarterly lists.)

Foxon, D. F. , ed. "English Bibliographical Sources"
[series title for primarily eighteenth-century catalogue reprints]. London: Gregg Press and Ar-
chive Press, 1964--. (This series was undertaken
as an attempt to fill the eighteenth-century gap in
British national bibliography--a period inadequate-
ly covered by Lowndes and Watt, entered below.
The series provides transcripts of contemporary
periodical lists of new publications, the list tran-
scribed varying with the period, e. g. , The Monthly Catalogue for 1714-1717, The Gentleman's Magazine 1731-51. "English Bibliographical Sources"
is, then, the raw material for a future eighteenth-
century STC.

Lowndes, William Thomas. The Bibliographer's Manual of English Literature, An Account of Rare,
Curious and Useful Books, Published in or Relating to Great Britain and Ireland, from the Inven-
tion of Printing; with Bibliographical and Critical
Notices, Collations of the Rare Articles, and
Prices at which They Have Been Sold [Caxton to
1820]. (Often inaccurate but useful as a supplement to the British Museum General Catalogue.)

Watt, Robert. Bibliotheca Britannica; or, A General
Index to British and Foreign Literature [Caxton
to 1824]. 4 vols. Edinburgh: N. Constable,
1824. (Like Lowndes, best used in conjunction
with the British Museum General Catalogue.)

The English Catalogue of Books ... [1801--]. London:

Sampson Low, 1864-1901; Publishers' Circular,
1906--. (Based on lists appearing in a trade
journal, the Publishers' Circular, now titled
British Books.)
Whitaker's Cumulative Book List: A Classified List
of Publications. London: J. Whitaker, 1924--.
(Cumulation of lists published in the trade jour-
nals The Bookseller and Current Literature.)
The British National Bibliography. London: Council
of the British National Bibliography, 1950--.
(Considered the best current national bibliography.)
British Books in Print: The Reference Catalogue of
Current Literature. London: J. Whitaker, 1874--.
(Prior to 1966, BBIP was known by its subtitle.)
Cumulative Book Index: A World List of Books in the
English Language. (S56).

3. Also included are all Latin service-books, wherever
printed, between 1475 and 1640, for use in England
and Scotland.

4. If no place of publication is given, the work was published in London. A query after the note of entry
refers not to the date but to the identity of the book.

5. Works listed are being made available on microfilm;
see Early English Books 1475-1640 (Ann Arbor, Mich.:
University Microfilms, [1938--]). A cross-index to
completed reels was published under the same title in
1972.

M25. Evans, Charles. American Bibliography: A Chronological Dictionary of All Books, Pamphlets, and
Periodical Publications Printed in the United
States of America from the Genesis of Printing
in 1639 Down to and Including the Year 1820 with
Bibliographical and Biographical Notes. 12 vols.
1903-34; rpt. New York: Peter Smith, 1941;
rpt. in one volume--Metuchen, N.J.: Mini-Print
Corp., 1967. [Actually reaches only to 1799;
completed through 1800 by Clifford Shipton under
the title The American Bibliography of Charles
Evans ... (1955; rpt. Worcester, Mass.: American Antiquarian Society, 1962) and indexed by

Roger Pattrell Bristol under Shipton's title (Worcester, Mass.: American Antiquarian Society, 1959). Shipton and Bristol's additions constitute vols. XIII and XIV of "Evans."][1]

Like Pollard and Redgrave's Short-Title Catalogue (M24), Evans is a retrospective listing of the first works in a national bibliography. As such it is an invaluable source for studies in early American literature. Because of its chronological arrangement, this work may be regarded as a literary history in bibliographic form. The first few pages of Evans' preface make fascinating--often inspirational--reading. Here Evans not only presents a capsule history of the United States implicit in American printed documents but also movingly expresses the love of books and country that underlie his thirty-five year labor compiling the American Bibliography.

Contents:

1) Virtually all printed matter published in American between 1639 and 1800:[2] includes periodicals and newspapers under every year in which they were published.

2) Bibliographical information: full title and sub-title,[3] author's full name with birth and death dates, and bibliographic description including imprint [printer and/or publisher, and place and date of publication found at the bottom of the title page], paging, and format.[4]

3) Bibliographical and biographical annotation.

4) Some cursory locating of entries.[5]

5) Historical and literary surveys preceding Vols. I-V.

6) Author, subject, and printer indexes.

Arrangement:

1) Chronological; alphabetical by author's name within the year of publication, with anonymous works found under the probable author's name.[6]

2) Numbered entries: this "Evans number" is important for finding works listed in Evans, all of which are being made available in a microcard edition, Early American Imprints 1639-1800.

3) Separate author and subject indexes at the back of each volume.

4) Directory of printers and publishers at the back of Vols. I-XII, arranged by town in Vol. I, thereafter by state.

5) Comprehensive author-title index, Vol. XIV. Since names of people, ships, and Indian tribes appearing in titles are entered, to some extent Vol. XIV can also serve as a subject index. [7]

Review Questions:

1) Why does Evans call his work a "Dictionary"?

2) Through what year does its coverage extend?

3) In what respects is the American Bibliography similar to Pollard and Redgrave's STC? In what respects is it different?

4) Where are the indexes to Evans?

Research Problems:

1) What was the first work printed in America? Where was it printed, by whom, and in what form?

2) What were the first two Shakespearean plays printed in America? Where and when were they printed? When was Hamlet first printed in America? In what form was it printed? Was Paradise Lost printed in America before or after Hamlet?

3) How many publications dealing with the history of Rhode Island were printed in the United States in 1800?

Notes (Evans)

1. Further additions to Evans include Bristol's Index to Printers, Publishers, and Booksellers Indicated by Charles Evans in his American Bibliography (1961), his Supplement to Charles Evans' American Bibliography (1970), and his Index to Supplement ... (1971), all published by the University of Virginia Press. Also see Clifford K. Shipton and James E. Mooney, National Index of American Imprints Through 1800: The Short-Title Evans, 2 vols. ([Worcester, Mass.]: American Antiquarian Society and Barre Publishers, 1969).

2. Our American national bibliography can be constructed from the following works:

Sabin, Joseph. Bibliotheca Americana: A Dictionary of Books Relating to America, from its Discovery to the Present Time [to 1892] (S65).

Shaw, Ralph R., and Richard H. Shoemaker. American Bibliography: A Preliminary Checklist [1801-19]. 22 vols. New York: Scarecrow Press, 1958-66.

Roorbach, O. A. Bibliotheca Americana: Catalogue of American Publications 1820-[1861]. 4 vols. 1852-61; rpt. New York: Peter Smith, 1939; rpt. in one volume (with Kelly--see below)--Metuchen, N. J.: Mini-Print Corp., 1967. (Coverage of the years 1820-1830 is superseded by Shoemaker's Checklist below.)

Shoemaker, Richard H. A Checklist of American Imprints [1820-1830]. 12 vols. New York [later Metuchen, N. J.]: Scarecrow Press, 1964-72. [Vol. X (1830) comp. Gayle Cooper; Vols. XI and XII (indexes) comp. M. Francis Cooper.]

Kelly, James. The American Catalogue of Books [1861-71]. 2 vols. 1866-71; rpt. New York: Peter Smith, 1938; rpt. in one volume (with Roorbach--see above)--Metuchen, N. J.: Mini-Print Corp., 1967. (Many inaccuracies.)

Publishers' Weekly. New York, 1872--. (Can be used in conjunction with Sabin to fill the gap between Kelly and The American Catalogue of Books below.)

The American Catalogue of Books [1876-1910]. 13 vols. 1880-1911; rpt. New York: Peter Smith, 1941. (Based on lists of new books appearing in Publishers' Weekly.)

The Publishers' Trade List Annual. New York, 1873--. (Indexed since 1948 in Books in Print [M30a].)

Cumulative Book Index [1898--] (S56).

United States Catalogue. Minneapolis [later N. Y.]: H. W. Wilson, 1899--. (Replaced The American Catalogue of Books [1876-1910].)

American Book Publishing Record. New York: R. R. Bowker, 1960--.

3. But Shipton uses short titles in his Vol. XIII because of high printing costs.

4. Although Evans attempts to identify accurately every work and edition listed, American Bibliography, like its British counterparts, must be used warily.

5.   Evans' location initials are identified by John C. Munger
     in the New York Public Library Bulletin for August,
     1936.   In his preface to Vol. XIII of The American
     Bibliography, Shipton points out that Evans' minimal
     locating does not necessarily attest to the rarity of
     the books cited.

6.   Since Evans was often mistaken in his attributions, look
     up anonymous works by title in Bristol's author-title
     index (Vol. XIV).

7.   Newspapers and almanacs are listed not under their titles
     but under the headings "newspapers" and "almanacs, "
     under "N" and "A. "

Research Problems:

1) What is the literary importance of the Epistola Cuthberti de Obitu Bedae? What historical transformation is revealed by the poem it contains? Who has written the standard study of Cuthbert's letter? Where can you find a modern edition of the "Death Song"?

2) Using an annotated bibliography, discover the thesis of Alan Holder's "The Flintlocks of the Fathers: Robert Lowell's Treatment of the American Past" (1971). Cite full publication information for Holder's article.

3) How many important biographical, political, and critical treatments of Sir Walter Raleigh appeared in the seventeenth century? Where can you find a modern scholarly discussion of Raleigh's marriage?

4) What French, Italian, and Greek works influenced the Erotokritos? When was the Erotokritos first published? When was its importance first recognized? Whose translation is most recent?

5) What reference work is completely devoted to biographies of outstanding contemporary black Americans? When was it first published? How frequently is it published? As of 1970, what is the latest edition?

6) What was Faulkner's last novel? What is it about? What significant political and scientific events took place in the year of its publication?

7) Which British and American libraries and collectors hold original copies of the English translation of Ludwig Lavatar's "Of ghostes a. spirites walking by nyght" (printed 1572)? What other works by Lavatar were translated into English and published in the sixteenth century?

8) List the works of the scholar Merritt Hughes, published between 1965 and 1968. (Supply full bibliographical information, and explain all abbreviations.)

9) Under what title was the London edition of Harold Frederic's The Damnation of Theron Ware (an American novel) first issued? What was the British publisher's source for this title?

10) By quoting a few lines of verse, demonstrate and explain how the art of the American poetess Anne Bradstreet was adversely affected by her Puritan beliefs. Whose critical opinion are you following?

11) Prepare a primary bibliography of the plays of Maxwell Anderson (an American) published in the 1940's. Prepare a bibliography of critical articles about Winterset. (Explain all abbreviations.)

12) What two jokes did Sir Thomas More make just before his execution? In what work was More first associated with two other Catholic saints? (Cite place and year of publication.)

13) List all the bibliographies of George Eliot, regardless of the form in which they appeared, published between 1963 and 1967.

14) What are Sir Laurence Olivier's hobbies? When was he created Baron of Brighton? What role did he play in his first appearance, at the age of fifteen, at the Stratford-on-Avon Shakespeare Festival?

15) Which of Carson McCullers' works have been filmed? Which have been adapted for the stage? When did Carson McCullers die?

16) Henry V defeated the French at Agincourt on St. Crispin's Day. Where is Agincourt? On what day of the year was this battle fought? Who was St. Crispin? Identify the Shakespearean play, act, and scene in which this line occurs: "This day is call'd the feast of Crispian."

17) In what year was the first almanac printed in New England? The "Bay Psalm Book"? The first publication of Harvard College? The first spelling book?

18) What is "cubist poetry"? Name three poets whose writing could be described as "cubist."

19) Cite a bibliography published in 1937 of famous literary

works set in England's lake district. Of what series is
this bibliography a part? How many literary works are
entered? Account for the paucity of entries.

20) Cite an explicatory criticism of Browning's "Porphyria's
Lover. " (Supply full publication information for the
source you cite.)

21) In what sense was the year 1830 a turning point in German literary criticism? Under what modern rubric would
Bertolt Brecht's critical writings be listed? What philosophers have most markedly influenced modern German
criticism? Name the critic you are following.

22) What was the only work by Synesius of Cyrene to be
translated into English in the sixteenth century? Under
what title was it translated?

23) In 1964, John Barth wrote a piece for the New American
Library edition of a famous eighteenth-century novel.
Name the novel. What was Barth's contribution to this
edition? What other works by Barth were first published
in 1964?

24) Distinguish between two kinds of dirges in Greek literature. Name two Greek writers of dirges. What literary
work provides the earliest evidence for such dirges?

25) Does the OED have an entry for "trigger" used as a verb
in the sense of "to initiate or cause"? What conclusions
can you reach about "trigger" as a verb?

CHAPTER IV

ABSTRACTS, INDEXES, AND DIRECTORIES

M26.   Abstracts of English Studies

M27a.   Dissertation Abstracts International

M27b.   Comprehensive Dissertation Index

M28.   Essay and General Literature Index

M29.   Index to Book Reviews in the Humanities

M30a.   Books in Print

M30b.   Subject Guide to Books in Print

M31.   Ulrich's International Periodicals Directory

A compilation of abstracts may be regarded as an index that lists, locates, and, most important, briefly describes longer studies. Indexes, whether designed to analyze the contents of particular publications or to search miscellaneous publications for particular literary genres or subjects, are among the most important locating tools. A directory is essentially an alphabetically arranged listing of persons, places, organizations, or publications. Ulrich's is especially useful because it is both descriptive and classified. When one considers the enormous proliferation of literary publications in modern times, the value of abstracts, indexes, and directories becomes evident at once.

M26.   Abstracts of English Studies: An Official Publication
        of the National Council of Teachers of English.
        Boulder, Colo.: University of Colorado, 1958.

AES is a compilation of abstracts--short summaries--of periodical articles dealing with English language literature and the English language. Abstracts are time savers: on

the one hand, since the abstract user can quickly determine
which articles are relevant to his own special interest, he
need locate and read only those; on the other hand, abstracts
can help the user keep abreast of far more periodical literature than he could hope to read in its entirety.   Abstracts
are non-evaluative: AES abstracts "state the thesis, express
the method of development, and point to the major implica-
tions drawn by the articles" (Abstract Policy).   Other valuable abstracting services are American Literature Abstracts
(S67), MLA Abstracts (S66), and Dissertation Abstracts International (M27a).

Contents:

1)   Abstracts of periodical articles only; no books.
2)   Worldwide coverage: over a thousand periodicals
      screened. [1]
3)   General literary and linguistic studies, English, Com-
      monwealth, and American literature in English and
      related languages.
4)   Ten issues a year, cumulated annually. [2]
5)   Monthly indexes cumulated annually.

Arrangement:

1)   Categories (general, English, American, and world
      literature in English and related languages): serves
      as a guide to the order of abstract entries. [3]
2)   Key to abbreviations of journals abstracted in the
      particular issue of AES.
3)   Initialled and numbered abstract entries of about 150
      words. [4]
4)   Monthly index:
      a.   keyed to item, not page, numbers;
      b.   includes, in a single alphabet, author, anonymous
           title, and subject entries.
5)   Annual index:
      a.   includes sub-categories (e.g., the Shakespeare
           entries are broken down under separate title en-
           tries);
      b.   includes a separate index of authors of the arti-
           cles abstracted (as of 1968).

Review Questions:

1)   Does the abstracter attempt to judge the quality of the
      article he summarizes?

2)   What subject areas are covered by AES?

3)   Are books abstracted in AES?

4)   Name three other abstracting services.

5)   Do the indexes use page or item number references?

6)   Does the annual index contain entries for the authors of
     abstracted periodical articles?

Research Problems:

1)   Compile a list of articles on Thoreau's transcendenta-
     lism abstracted in AES during 1964. (Cite full biblio-
     graphical information for each.)

2)   Locate an abstract of Peter Ure's article on G. B.
     Shaw, published in April, 1969. What is the title of
     the article? In what periodical did it appear? Which
     four plays does Ure discuss? What is Shelleyan about
     these plays?

3)   Locate an abstract of Charles W. Smith's article in
     Papers on Language and Literature (Spring, 1966) on
     Gascoigne's The Adventures of Master F. J. How are
     the three inset stories related to The Adventures as a
     whole?

                        Notes (AES)

1.   As new journals are introduced, they are retrospectively
     abstracted.

2.   The abstract may not appear until several years after
     the publication of the article; therefore, if you cannot
     locate the abstract in the AES volume for the year of
     the article's publication, be certain to check more re-
     cent volumes of AES.

3.   Prior to September, 1969, abstracts were arranged
     alphabetically by title of the periodical in which they
     appeared.

4.   The names of the abstractors--Contributors to this Is-
     sue of AES--can be found on the inside back cover
     of the particular issue.

M27a.   Dissertation Abstracts International: Abstracts of
        Dissertations Available on Microfilm or as Xero-
        graphic Reproductions. [Ann Arbor]: Xerox Univer-
        sity Microfilms, 1938--. [Formerly Microfilm Ab-
        stracts (1938-51); Dissertation Abstracts (1952-69).]

M27b.   Comprehensive Dissertation Index 1861-1972.   37
        vols.   Ann Arbor: Xerox University Microfilms,
        1973.   [Annual supplements.]

DAI is a monthly compilation of abstracts (about 500
words) of American, Canadian, and a few foreign doctoral
dissertations.   These abstracts allow the student to keep
abreast of doctoral research in a particular area.   He may
purchase from Xerox University Microfilms a microfilmed or
xeroxed copy of any dissertation abstracted.

The CDI, a keyword-in-title and author index, makes
the finding of abstracts almost effortless.   An average of
six principal words in the dissertation title are indexed alphabetically.   For example, if one wishes to locate a dissertation on the roots of George Moore's realistic novels,
he may check either "roots," "Moore," or "realistic" in the
Literature and Language volumes of CDI; under any of these
he will find an entry for William Perkins' "George Moore's
Realistic Novels: Roots, Achievements, Influence" (Stanford,
1954, 526pp.) with reference to the volume, issue, and page
number of Dissertation Abstracts in which the abstract appears.   (The same information can also be found under "Perkins" in CDI's author index volumes.)   Because coverage extends from the very first Ph.D. dissertations written in
America to the present time and also includes locating entries for most non-abstracted dissertations, CDI eliminates
the need to search indexes in more specialized works. [1]

The following descriptions and review questions are
based on the 1973-74 volume of DAI and on the first 1973
edition of CDI.

Contents (DAI):

1)   Abstracts of dissertations written at over three hun-
     dred American and Canadian institutions (and a few
     foreign ones as well). [2]
2)   Relevant information: author, title, university,
     year of acceptance, supervisor (in some cases),
     length, and order number. [3]
3)   Indexes: both Keyword Title Index and Author Index
     for each monthly issue, [4] cumulated annually.

Arrangement (each issue of DAI):

1) Division into two parts:
   Part A--Humanities;
   Part B--Sciences (division begins with Vol. XXVII,
   no. 1 (July, 1966). [5]

2) Ordering information for copies of master's theses
   and doctoral dissertations, p. vi. [6]

3) Table of Contents (an alphabetically ordered subject
   classification), p. vii.

4) Abstract entries: within the broad subject heading
   (see Table of Contents) arranged alphabetically by
   author of dissertation.

5) Keyword title index followed by author index. [7]

Contents and Arrangement (CDI--Literature and Language
   vols. and author index):

1) Literature and Language: Vols. XXIX (A-L) and XXX
   (M-Z).

2) Clarification of keyword entry style and sample entries, pp. xi-xiv. [8]

3) Schools Included, p. xv.

4) Keyword index: arranged alphabetically by keyword;
   note cross-references to related broad subject head-
   ings--e.g., Biography and Theatre, both in Vol.
   XXXI--at the beginning of the Language and Literature
   volume.

5) Relevant information: under the keyword entry--title,
   author, degree, year awarded, conferring institution,
   length of dissertation, locating reference, and order
   number (if available from Xerox University Microfilms).

6) Author index, Vols. XXXIII-XXXVII. Alphabetically
   arranged by last name of author; entries duplicate
   those in (5) above.

Review Questions:

1) How "international" is DAI's coverage?

2) When did this abstracting service originate?

3) What is the current price of a paperbound xerographic
   copy of any abstracted dissertation?

4) What subject matter is covered in Part A of DAI?

5) How are dissertations arranged within Part A?

6) Does CDI index only those dissertations abstracted in DAI?

7) Which volumes of CDI cover Literature and Language?

8) How does a keyword-in-title index work?

9) Which volumes of CDI contain the cumulative author index?

Research Problems:

1) Cite a dissertation dealing with the reception of Balzac's novels in nineteenth-century America. Which American writers did Balzac influence?

2) Name a dissertation written prior to 1971 dealing with the sources of J. R. R. Tolkien's The Lord of the Rings and a dissertation dealing with its structure. Cite the authors' names, the schools conferring their degrees, and the length of the dissertations.

3) On what subjects did these eminent scholar-critics write their doctoral dissertations: Fredson T. Bowers? Maynard Mack? Robert Ornstein? If no order number for the dissertation abstract is given, note the source of your editor's citation.

Notes (DAI-CDI)

1. However, because of their foreign coverage, the student may still profitably consult the following works:
   Altick, Richard D., and William R. Matthews. Guide to Dissertations in Victorian Literature 1886-1958. Urbana: University of Illinois Press, 1960.
   Index to Theses Accepted for Higher Degrees by the Universities of Great Britain and Ireland and the Council for National Academic Awards [1950--]. London: ASLIB, 1953--.
   McNamee, Lawrence F. Dissertations in English and American Literature: Theses Accepted by American, British and German Universities, 1865-1964. New York: R. R. Bowker, 1968. Supplements.

Mikhail, E. H. Dissertations on Anglo-Irish Drama: A Bibliography of Studies 1870-1970. Totowa, N. J.: Rowman and Littlefield, 1973.

Woodress, James. Dissertations in American Literature, 1891-1966. 3rd ed. Durham, N. C.: Duke University Press, 1968. (Research in Progress-- a list of dissertations currently being written-- can be found immediately preceding the Bibliography section of the scholarly journal American Literature.)

2. Contributing institutions are listed on the front and back inside covers. Although the number of contributing institutions, beginning with an initial five in 1938, has only gradually increased, later participants often allowed microfilming of older dissertations. Hence CDI may cite an order number for a dissertation not abstracted in DAL.

3. Prior to 31 January 1971, the prices of xeroxed and microfilmed copies of dissertations varied with length and were, accordingly, entered under the abstract. Since the above date, prices of all dissertations have been standardized at $4.00 for a microfilmed copy, $10.00 for a paperbound xerographed copy, and $12.25 for a clothbound xerographed copy.

4. These annual cumulations constitute the supplements to CDI.

5. "The A and B sections are paginated separately and may be identified by the letters A or B following the page number" (Introduction).

6. For abstracts of master's theses, see Masters Abstracts: A Catalog of Selected Masters Theses on Microfilm (Ann Arbor: Xerox University Microfilms, 1962--). Dorothy M. Black, Guide to Lists of Master's Theses (Chicago: American Library Association, 1965) locates compilations of lists of American theses written earlier than 1962. Index to Theses Accepted for Higher Degrees by the Universities of Great Britain and Ireland ... (see above, note 1) is an annual title list of British master's theses and doctoral dissertations, with locating annotations.

For stylistic conventions observed in most master's theses and doctoral dissertations, see The MLA Style Sheet (S32).

7. The CDI and its forthcoming supplements supersede all
    previous indexes to DAI.

8. Under Explanation of Entries--Citations (p. xiv) the edi-
    tors note, "The prefix L. W. or X. indicates that
    the citation to the dissertation was obtained from
    American Doctoral Dissertations and its predeces-
    sors ... See the list of Sources Consulted [pp. xviii-
    xx] for complete information. "

M28. Essay and General Literature Index 1900-1933: An
      Index to Above 40, 000 Essays and Articles in
      2144 Volumes of Collections of Essays and Mis-
      cellaneous Works. Ed. Minnie Earl Sears and
      Marian Shaw. New York: H. W. Wilson, 1934.
      Supplements: 1934-69 (Vols. II-VII); thereafter,
      semiannual supplements bound annually and cumu-
      lated every five years.

        EGLI is a subject and author index to essays in books,
including essays originally published in periodicals and those
originally published as parts of books. It is especially valuable as an analyzing tool for Festschriften (volumes of essays in honor of an eminent scholar), similar collections of
essays on a variety of subjects, and chapters on disparate
subjects in books. [1] EGLI is also useful to the student of
literature in that it provides up-to-date primary and secondary bibliographies of essays for a given author. The author's essays are both listed and located as are critical essays on both his work in general and on individual works.

Contents:

    1)   Essays in books published from 1900 to date; thus
         essays written prior to 1900 are indexed if they have
         been reprinted in a twentieth-century volume.
    2)   Essays in all fields; biography and criticism stressed.
    3)   Unannotated. [2]
    4)   English language essays only; however, foreign lan-
         guage essays translated into English are included.
    5)   Generally indexes books by American publishers only;
         a few British editions are included.

Arrangement:

1) Abbreviations of periodical titles at front through Vol.
   III; thereafter periodical titles are given in full within
   the entry. [3]
2) Each volume arranged alphabetically, combining author,
   subject, and cross-reference entries. (Some title entries appear, enabling the student to locate an essay
   whose author is unknown to him.)
3) Under author entries EGLI lists in this order:
   a. works by the author.
   b. works about the author and his canon.
   c. criticisms of individual works. [4]
4) Cross-references from pseudonyms and subjects.
5) Subject entries arranged alphabetically by author within the subheading.
6) List of Books Indexed (citing full bibliographical information except for place of publication) at back of
   each volume; arranged alphabetically by author, editor,
   and title, with cross-references to the main entry.
7) From Vol. VII on, Directory of Publishers and Dis-
   tributors follows List of Books Indexed.

Review Questions:

1) For which of the following would you expect to find entries:
   a. an essay by Thomas Babington Macaulay, published
      in 1843?
   b. an article on Tennessee Williams in the Atlantic?
   c. an essay on Williams, in a collection entitled The
      Sound of Self-Parody, treating Albee, Miller, and
      Williams?
   d. the titles of all the chapters in a book by a single
      author, each chapter dealing with a different subject?
   e. an essay in French by Jean-Paul Sartre, published
      in a collection of essays?
   f. a chapter treating John Updike's Rabbit, Run?
   g. an essay in English analyzing the work of Aleksandr
      Solzhenitsyn?
   h. F. R. Leavis' essay, the title of which escapes you,
      on Othello?

2) Which of the following does EGLI contain:
   a. annotations for the essays indexed?

   b.   full bibliographical information for all books whose chapters are indexed?

   c.   subject headings and subdivisions?

   d.   cross-references from a pseudonym to the author's real name?

   e.   indexing of an essay published separately as a monograph?

   f.   clues as to whether an essay is by or about the author it is listed under?

   g.   a list of all the essays an author has written for a single collection?

Research Problems:

1)   Locate an essay in an anthology published between 1960-64 on the epic hero Beowulf and the newly discovered ship, the Sutton Hoo. What is the full name of the essayist and the title of the essay? Cite the title of the anthology, the full name of its editor, the publisher, and date of publication. On what pages of this anthology does the essay appear?

2)   In the thirty years since his death, have the essays of Paul Valéry (1871-1945) on the general subject of poetry been translated into English and collected in a single volume? If so, supply the title of this volume, its translator, and the name of the critic who wrote its introduction. What is the title of the collected edition and the volume number in which these essays were published? Of what series is the collected edition a part? Cite its series volume number.

3)   Locate the author of an essay on the English language entitled "English in 2061: A Forecast," published in a collection in the 1960's. Cite the title and editor of the collection, as well as the edition, the publisher, and the date of publication.

Notes (EGLI)

1.   For periodical articles later anthologized, EGLI may be considered a successor to Poole's Index to Periodical Literature 1802-[1905] (S74), The "A. L. A." [American Library Association] Index to General Literature, 2nd ed. (Boston: Houghton Mifflin, 1901), and The Nineteenth Century Reader's Guide (S75). Also see

Social Sciences and Humanities Index (S68) which analyzes the contents of modern British and American
scholarly journals; the British Humanities Index (S69)
which analyzes additional British journals; the Index
to [American] Little Magazines (S70), and the Index to
Commonwealth Little Magazines (S71). For indexes
to criticism, see checklist entry (M20, n. 1) and Cumulated Dramatic Index 1909-1949, 2 vols. (Boston:
G. K. Hall, 1965). For biography and bibliography,
see Biography Index (S40) and Bibliographic Index
(M18).

Other important indexes for locating primary
sources include the following:
Samples, Gordon H. The Drama Scholars' Index to
      Plays and Filmscripts: A Guide to Plays and
      Filmscripts in Selected Anthologies, Series, and
      Periodicals. Metuchen, N. J.: Scarecrow Press,
      1974.
Connor, John M., and Billie M. Connor. Ottemiller's
      Index to Plays in Collections [1900-1970]. 5th ed.
      rev. and enl. Metuchen, N. J.: Scarecrow Press,
      1971.
Play Index [1949-67 to date]. New York: H. W. Wil-
      son, 1953---. (Covers plays in collections and
      periodicals.)
Granger's Index to Poetry. Ed. William F. Bern-
      hardt. 5th ed. rev. and enl. New York: Colum-
      bia University Press, 1962. Supplement [through
      1965]. (Indexes anthologies.)
Short Story Index: An Index to 60, 000 Stories in
      4, 320 Collections. Comp. Dorothy E. Cook and
      Isabel S. Munro. New York: H. W. Wilson,
      1953. Supplements [1950--].

2.   Nevertheless, readers can often determine the nature of
     an essay cited as part of a book by 1) the subject
     heading assigned it, 2) the editors' use of the word
     "About" for biographical essays, 3) the designation
     "Criticism" for literary analyses, or 4) a separate
     listing under the individual literary work with which
     the essay deals.

3.   Periodical citations refer to the original publication
     source of an essay later included in a book.

4.   For collections of miscellaneous essays by a single au-
     thor, EGLI lists all the essays under the author's

name, followed by the title of the book. The word
"Contents" heads the lists of essays cited.

M29. Index to Book Reviews in the Humanities. Detroit:
         Philip Thomson, 1960--.

Reviewers usually perform three functions: description,
interpretation, and evaluation. Thus, a particular review
may serve as an introduction to a book, and a census of reviews may serve as an indicator of that book's reception by
the author's contemporaries. Reviews in scholarly journals
are especially important as guides to the accuracy, thorough-
ness, and depth of secondary studies and reference works.
IBRH analyzes more literary periodicals than any other index
of twentieth-century book reviews. [1] Reviews of both creative
work and secondary studies are located.

Contents:

1) Currently lists all book reviews in scholarly humani-
     ties periodicals and in a number of general interest
     periodicals. [2]
2) Annual.
3) Non-cumulative.
4) Current subject coverage: Art and Architecture,
     Biography, Dance and Drama, Folklore, Language,
     Literature, Music, Philosophy, Travel, Adventure.
5) Language of books reviewed and of the reviews them-
     selves generally English, but a few in German,
     French, and Italian.
6) Reviews of important new editions of older books. [3]
7) Length of indexed reviews usually about a page. [3]
8) Bibliographical information about books reviewed:
     generally only author and/or editor, title, and titles
     under which the book has been published abroad.
     Translations are cited only when necessary for identi-
     fication, e.g., translations of Homer's Odyssey.
9) Unannotated entries.
10) Currency of publication: the Index is published ap-
     proximately six months following the year in which
     the reviews appeared. [4]

Arrangement:

1) Prefatory pages explaining changes in converage.

2) Common abbreviations.
3) List of periodicals in which reviews appear: for each periodical, the Index provides a code number and cites place of publication, stated frequency of publication, and the timespan covered by the volumes of the periodical analyzed in the particular volume of the Index. Abbreviations of periodical titles correspond to those in the MLA International Bibliography (M7).
4) Reviews entered alphabetically by author of the book;[5] within the listing for each book, alphabetically by reviewer's name.
5) Review information includes reviewer's name when known, code number of the periodical in which the review appears (identified at the front of the IBRH volume), the date, and the page.

Review Questions:

1) For which of the following would you expect to find review citations in IBRH:
   a. a Josephine Tey mystery?
   b. The Sensuous Woman by "J"?
   c. a 1962 study of Catholic doctrine?
   d. a short story from the New Yorker?
   e. Religious Rite and Ceremony in Milton's Poetry?
   f. a French edition of Mozart's librettos?
   g. Gestaltung und Gestalten in modernen Drama (1968)?
   h. a French translation of Nabokov's Lolita?
   i. De Felice's biography Mussolini il Fascista?
   j. a recent review in the New Statesman of a book entitled Economics in an African Society?

2) Which of these would the Index include:
   a. a review you read in the Los Angeles Times?
   b. the place of publication for journals cited?
   c. the length of the review?
   d. annotation following the review citation?
   e. the year in which the review appeared in a journal?
   f. a review for a British book whose title was changed for publication in the United States?
   g. review citations for the same book in more than one annual volume of the Index?
   h. a generally high level of scholarly reviewing?

3) Could you locate a review in the Index if you knew only the title of the book and its reviewer?

Research Problems:

1) How many signed book reviews of Mary Renault's his-
    torical novel The Mask of Apollo are listed in IBRH for
    1966, the year of the novel's publication? Has Peter
    Wolfe's Twayne Series study of Mary Renault (1969) at-
    tracted much critical attention?

2) How many reviews of the fourth edition of James D.
    Hart's The Oxford Companion to American Literature
    appeared in the 1960's? (That is, how many are cited
    in the Index to Book Reviews in the Humanities?) When
    and where did they appear? What else was Hart evident-
    ly working on during this same decade?

3) Book reviewers frequently have wide ranging interests.
    What single critic reviewed the books listed below:
    Kingsley Amis' The James Bond Dossier, Andrew Sharp's
    A Green Tree in Gedde, Randolph S. Churchill's Twenty-
    One Years, Charles Chaplin's My Autobiography, Fran-
    çoise Gilot's Life With Picasso? In what periodical did
    his reviews appear? Is there an MLA abbreviation of
    the title of this periodical?

Notes (IBRH)

1. For nineteenth-century book reviews, see Poole's Index
    (S74), Nineteenth Century Reader's Guide (S75), and
    The Wellesley Index (S76). Alternatives to IBRH--
    indexes to twentieth-century reviews--are Book Re-
    view Digest (S73) and Book Review Index (S72). Re-
    views are also listed in the Index to Little Magazines
    (S70) and the Index to Commonwealth Little Magazines
    (S71). For reviews of scholarly/critical works, also
    see the Annual Bibliography of English Language and
    Literature (S44). For reviews of books too recent to
    have been indexed, consult the New York Times Book
    Review, and The Times Literary Supplement (a sec-
    tion of the London Times).

2. Over six hundred periodical and annual titles are ex-
    amined and indexed. However, periodicals primarily
    concerned with the social sciences are no longer in-
    dexed in IBRH.

3. Book Review Digest (S73) provides the actual word length
    for readers in search of a more substantial analysis.

4. Since reviews often appear quite belatedly in scholarly
    journals, readers should examine a number of volumes
    of the Index. Beginning with the 1963 volume, an
    asterisk designates book reviews also cited in preced-
    ing volumes. Beginning with the 1965 volume, the
    year of the review is given in each citation; in pre-
    ceding volumes, generally the year is listed only when
    it differs from the year being indexed.

5. The name used on the title page of the book is the des-
    ignation under which each entry will be found, regard-
    less of whether it is the author's real name or a
    pseudonym.

M30a. Books in Print 1974. 4 vols. New York: R. R.
       Bowker, 1974. (Originated in 1948 as An Author-
       Title-Series Index to the Publishers' Trade List
       Annual.)[1]

M30b. Subject Guide to Books in Print 1974. 2 vols. New
       York: R. R. Bowker, 1974. (Originated in
       1957.)

       BIP may be regarded as one form of the current
American national bibliography; from 1948 on, it has provided an annual listing of most of the books published and/
or distributed in the United States. [2] Every attempt is made
to list all available books. In consequence, BIP can be
found in virtually all bookstores and libraries, however small.
Information regarding the price of various editions of a book
is particularly useful to instructors choosing required texts
for their students. [3] Volumes I and II of BIP are an author
index; Vols. III and IV, a title index.
       The following description, review questions, and re-
search problems are based on BIP and its Subject Guide for
1974.

Contents (BIP):

1) Almost all hardcover books in print: includes trade
    books, textbooks, and juveniles. [4]
2) Many but not all paperbacks; none under thirty-five
    pages are included. [5]
3) Books forthcoming within the year. [6]
4) Full ordering information: includes author (or editor,

compiler, translator), title, price, publisher, series,
and language.
5)   Cross-references from co-authors, co-editors, and
various forms of an author's name.
6)   Publishers' addresses.

Arrangement (BIP, Vols. I and II):

1)   [Vol. I] How to Use BIP (see for M', Mc, Mac entries and any difficulties encountered with initials or
abbreviations).
2)   [Vol. I] Key to basic abbreviations.
3)   Author index: alphabetically arranged by last name
of author, (Vol. I, A-J, and Vol. II, K-Z).

Arrangement (BIP, Vols. III and IV):

1)   Title index (Vol. III, A-J, and Vol. IV, K-Z).
2)   [Vol. IV] Key to Publishers' Abbreviations used in
BIP: a directory of addresses.
3)   [Vol. IV] Directory of Publishers in the U.S.:   addresses and telephone numbers of all active American publishers.

Contents (Subject Guide to BIP):

1)   All books in print (including biographical and historical
fiction) suitable for entry under a subject heading,
generally LC; single works of fiction, poetry, and
drama not lending themselves to a subject approach
should be looked up in BIP.
2)   Entries duplicate those in BIP.

Arrangement (Subject Guide, Vol. I):

1)   Directions for use.
2)   Key to basic abbreviations.
3)   Key to Publishers' Abbreviations: includes addresses.
4)   Subject entries: A-J.

Arrangement (Subject Guide, Vol II):

1)   Subject entries: K-Z.

Review Questions:

1)   Are periodicals entered in BIP or in the Subject Guide?

2)   Does BIP list every published paperbound book?

3) What information does BIP provide that is especially useful for instructors choosing an edition of a classic for
class use?

4) Could you learn from BIP whether a work was available
in the 1950's?

5) If a work is not currently in print, where would you try
to locate it?

6) Which volumes of BIP are the author index?

7) For books dealing with Chaucer's sources, would you
look in Volumes I, II, III, or IV of BIP or in the Subject Guide to BIP?

Research Problems:

1) Which of these books were in print in 1974: G. B. Har-
rison's Profession of English, E. M. W. Tillyard's
Shakespeare's History Plays, A. C. Bradley's Shakespearean Tragedy, Sinclair Lewis' Ann Vickers? Which
were available in paperback?

2) How many collections of nineteenth-century English drama
were in print in 1974? Which of these is devoted to
melodrama? Cite the price, the publisher, and his address.

3) As of 1974, name the most recent in-print, annotated
bibliography of literary criticism devoted to the works
of Thomas Hardy. Of what series is this bibliography
a part? Cite the publisher and his address.

Notes (BIP)

1. The Publishers' Trade List Annual (New York: R. R.
Bowker, 1873--), a yearly collection of American publishers' catalogs, may be used to discover what works
are part of a publisher's series, since BIP is no
longer a series index. For works that are part of a
series (but not a publisher's series), see Titles in
Series (S78). Some series that repay acquaintance
include "Studies in English Literature, " "Writers and
Critics, " "English Men of Letters, " "Twentieth-Century Views, " "Writers and Their Work, " "University
of Minnesota Pamphlets on American Writers, "

"Goldentree Bibliographies in Language and Literature, " "Soho Bibliographies, " "Serif Series: Bibliographies and Checklists, " and "Charles E. Merrill Checklists. "

2. For the reference components of an American national bibliography from its beginnings to the present, see Evans' American Bibliography (M25), Sabin's Bibliotheca Americana (S65), and the Cumulative Book Index (S56).

3. Although publishers attempt to anticipate price changes (as well as books soon to be in print or out), Bowker's BIP Supplement should be consulted for interim changes.

4. Omitted are government publications, most professional law books, Spanish language books distributed in the U.S.A., subscription reference sets, book club editions, and periodicals or other non-books. Books that may become unavailable during the year are excluded whenever possible.

5. Bowker's Paperbound Books in Print (1955), published triannually, lists not only paperbacks for which there is a hardback edition but also books published only as paperbacks.

6. A separate bimonthly publication, Bowker's Forthcoming Books (1966--), provides author-title indexes to all books scheduled to appear within the next five months. Its companion publication is Subject Guide to Forthcoming Books (1967--).

M31. [Carolyn F.] Ulrich's International Periodicals Directory: A Classified Guide to Current Periodicals, Foreign and Domestic. 15th ed. New York: R. R. Bowker, 1973-74.

Ulrich's, the most comprehensive listing of periodicals and periodical information available, is especially useful as a guide to American and British magazines. New editions and supplements are published biennially in alternating years.

Contents:

1) Periodicals in almost all subject areas.

2) Periodicals in many languages; foreign language titles are annotated, i. e., the contents are described.

3) Current periodicals: discontinued periodicals are entered under Cessations. [1]

4) Periodicals published more frequently than once a year. [2]

5) The weekly supplements and editions of some major newspapers are included.

6) Special features noted: reviews of books, films, etc.; abstracts, bibliographies, languages used in the text, [3] annual index, cumulative indexes, and the names of indexing and/or abstracting services (e. g., Reader's Guide to Periodical Literature) that analyze the contents of the particular periodical.

7) Full bibliographic publishing information: editor's name, address, price of subscription, etc. [4]

Arrangement:

1) Preliminary sections include Abbreviations, Abstracting and Indexing Services, and a broad Key to Subjects in English with French, German, and Spanish equivalents.

2) The directory proper: periodicals classified by subject. As of the 1969 edition, the broad subject headings are arranged in alphabetical order; within the subject heading, periodical titles are also listed alphabetically. (The headings "Linguistics and Philology," "Literary and Political Reviews," and "Literature, General and Poetry" are particularly relevant.)

3) Cross-references:
   a. to main entries by italicized page numbers, and
   b. to subject headings under which journals of similar interest may be found.

4) Index to New Periodicals (periodicals that have appeared within the last three years).

5) Cessations: periodicals recently discontinued.

6) Title and Subject Index.

Review Questions:

1) Which of the following would you expect to find included in a recent edition of Ulrich's:
   a. journals published in India, Japan, or Latin America?
   b. journals dealing with ecology? with black theatre?
   c. Mad Magazine?

    d.   The nineteenth-century Edinburgh Review, no longer
         published?
    e.   cross-references to broad subject headings?

2)   Which of the following could Ulrich's be used to find:
    a.   all the journals devoted to a specific subject, e.g.,
         Poetry?
    b.   which abstracting or indexing service contains en-
         tries for a particular journal?
    c.   an abstract of an article from a journal?
    d.   information necessary for the would-be subscriber
         to a particular journal?
    e.   information necessary for the would-be contributor
         to a particular journal?
    f.   a cumulative index for a particular journal?

Research Problems:

1)   Locate a periodical dealing with linguistic usage in the
    United States, which is 1) indexed in the Social Sciences
    and Humanities Index, and which 2) contains book reviews
    of current publications in its field. What university pub-
    lishes this journal? When was this journal first pub-
    lished?

2)   To what subject is the Baker Street Journal devoted?
    What organization sponsors the journal? How wide is its
    circulation?

3)   What is the name of the association that publishes the
    MLA International Bibliography of Books and Articles on
    the Modern Languages and Literatures? How many sub-
    scribers does this bibliography have? How much would
    it cost a member of the association to receive one part
    of the four-part annual bibliography?

Notes (Ulrich's)

1.   Regarding discontinued periodicals, Constance Winchell
     notes that "earlier issues [of Ulrich's] may be useful,
     both for the listing of periodicals no longer published
     and for special lists included, e.g.: A list of clan-
     destine periodicals of World War II, by Adrienne
     Florence Muzzy, in the 5th ed. 1947" (p. 135). In-
     cidentally, it should be noted that discontinued or
     arcane periodicals mentioned in Ulrich's can be lo-

cated in American libraries through the Union List of
Serials (S79) or New Serial Titles (S79, passim).

2. For periodicals published annually, less frequently than
    once a year, or irregularly, consult Irregular Serials
    and Annuals (S80). Both this work and Ulrich's are
    kept up-to-date by Bowker Serials Bibliography Supple-
    ment (New York: R. R. Bowker, 1972--), published
    biennially in the years between editions of the major
    directories. The usefulness of the 1972 Supplement
    can be gauged from the fact that it contains 6,500
    titles not included in the previous editions of the di-
    rectories.

3. The language of the periodical is the language of the
    country of publication unless otherwise indicated.

4. For further information useful to the would-be contributor
    to a particular literary periodical, consult Gersten-
    berger and Hendrick's Third Directory of Periodicals
    (S81) and The MLA Style Sheet (M32).

CHAPTER V

SOME AUXILIARY TOOLS

M32. Variorum: The Variorum Edition of the Plays of
        W. B. Yeats
M33. Concordance: Concordance to the Plays of W. B.
        Yeats
M34. Familiar Quotations
M35a. The Library of Literary Criticism
M35b. The Critical Temper
M36a. The New Encyclopaedia Britannica
M36b. Britannica Book of the Year

        Chapter V introduces a number of miscellaneous works,
all of importance to the student of literature. A variorum
edition presents all the extant versions of a particular work
and often provides a compendium of criticism on that work
as well. A concordance may be regarded as an index to the
words an author uses. Bartlett's, though chronologically arranged, is actually an index of famous quotations. Moulton's
Library of Literary Criticism and its successors serve both
as surveys and indexes to important interpretations of literature. Britannica, still the outstanding multi-volumed general
encyclopedia, may best be used as an initial source for extra-
literary information.

M32. The Variorum Edition of the Plays of W. B. Yeats.
        Ed. Russell K. Alspach. New York: Macmillan,
        1966.

        Alspach's work is an example of the modern variorum
edition. Although Alspach deals with one genre within the
author's canon, a variorum editor may limit himself to only

102

a single work or may treat an author's entire canon. The
value of the modern variorum is two-fold: presenting variant
versions both reveals the development of a work and also al-
lows the reader to choose among alternate readings where
the writer's final choice is uncertain. Older variorum editions contain not only variant readings but line-by-line critical
annotations by famous commentators; see, for example, A New
Variorum Edition of Shakespeare, ed. Horace Howard Furness (Philadelphia: J. B. Lippincott, 1871--), now in 23
volumes with continuing bibliographical supplements issued
under the auspices of the Modern Language Association of
America.

Contents:

1) Basic text of the plays: based on the London Macmillan edition of The Collected Plays of W. B. Yeats
   (1952); numbered lines.
2) List of all significant printings of the plays.
3) Line-by-line entering of all variant versions (changes,
   additions, and deletions in words and punctuation),
   citing the printings in which the variants occur.
4) Reprinting of the original version of plays revised so
   drastically as to preclude intelligible collation with
   later versions.
5) Yeats' prefaces, dedications, and notes to the plays
   collated with their variant versions.

Arrangement:

1) Table of Contents, pp. xvii-xviii.
2) Bibliography, pp. xix-xxiv: the editions collated listed
   chronologically and numbered for cross-reference to
   the variant readings.
3) The Collations, p. xxv: explanation of symbols, abbreviations, and method used.
4) The plays: the page is divided by a horizontal line
   with the basic text printed above the line, the variants
   below it; when Alspach reprints the original version of
   a play, it appears on the verso (left-hand) pages only.
5) Yeats' notes to a particular play printed at the end of
   that play; cross-references to other notes.
6) Appendix I: Yeats' general notes.
7) Appendix II: Yeats' Prefaces and Dedications, primarily from the plays.
8) Appendix III: Dates, Places of Performance, and
   Casts of Characters of First Productions.

9)   Index, Part I: alphabetical list of characters citing
the play in which the character appears and the line
in both the basic text and the variants where he first
speaks.   Part II, General Index.

Review Questions:

1)   What is the difference between a modern variorum edition and an older one like Furness' New Variorum Edition of Shakespeare?

2)   Of what value is a variorum edition?

3)   Why are the lines of the variorum text numbered?

4)   How is the basic text separated from the variant readings?

5)   How do you use Alspach's Bibliography?

Research Problems:

1)   Which of the following plays did Yeats revise the most
and which the least: Sophocles' King Oedipus: A Version for the Modern Stage; The Unicorn from the Stars;
The Countess Cathleen?   What were the original production conditions that influenced Yeats' purpose and style
in his King Oedipus?

2)   What does Yeats have to say about the Elizabethan stage
in contrast to the modern theatre?

3)   In which version of Yeats' In Baile's Strand are these
lines found?
197.   I think that a fierce woman's better, a woman
198.   That breaks away when you have thought her won,
199.   For I'd be fed and hungry at one time.
Does Yeats keep this passage in any later versions of
the play?   How do you know?

M33.   A Concordance to the Plays of W. B. Yeats.   Ed.
Eric Domville.   2 vols.   Ithaca: Cornell University Press, 1972.

Domville's work is an example of a computer-produced

concordance. A concordance is an alphabetical index of all
words used in the work or works treated, citing the line in
which they occur. A concordance can be based on a single
work, e.g., Byron's Don Juan, ed. Charles W. Hagelman,
Jr. and Robert J. Barnes (Ithaca: Cornell University Press,
1967); on one or more genres within an author's canon, as
is the work at hand; or an author's entire literary output,
e.g., A Concordance to the Writings of William Blake, ed.
David V. Erdman, 2 vols. (Ithaca: Cornell University Press,
1967). The most frequent uses of a concordance are to determine the author's vocabulary, to discover the various
senses in which he uses a word, to discover words characteristic of his style, to find a work's imagery patterns as
reflected in the high frequency of particular words, and to
help locate a partly forgotten passage.

Prior to 1955, concordances were prepared manually;
in consequence, listed words are usually quoted in a lengthier
and more intelligible context. See, for example, A Concordance to the Poems of Edmund Spenser, ed. Charles Grosvenor
Osgood (1915; rpt. Gloucester, Mass.: Peter Smith, 1963).

Contents:

1) All the words in the plays and in significant variant
   lines, cited in the context of the line; this concordance is based upon Alspach's Variorum Edition of the
   Plays (M32).
2) Excludes names of speakers, stage directions, and
   such nonsignificant words as a, am, an, etc.
3) Frequency count of words entered.

Arrangement:

1) Preface: list of omitted words, I, x; explanation of
   line numbering, I, xi-xii; list of abbreviations, I,
   xiii-xiv; explanation of variant entries, I, xiv-xv.
2) Alphabetical entries: the concordance proper.
3) Appendix: Index of words in order of frequency, II,
   1533-58; the list is headed by words used most frequently and ends with words used only once.

Review Questions:

1) Specify some of the uses of a concordance.

2) Why is it important to know what text the concordance
   is based upon?

3)   What main classes of words does Domville omit from his concordance?

4)   What does the Appendix contain?

Research Problems:

Concordance and Variorum:

1)   This line begins the last song of one of Yeats' plays: "The wind blows out of the gates of the day ... " Quote the rest of the song.   In what play does it appear?

2)   In which of his plays does Yeats use the word "dreamless"?   Quote the intelligible context (two lines or more) in which this word occurs.

Concordance

3)   Note the frequencies of the following words in Yeats' plays: old 527, God 380, heart 259, dead 225, death 185.   Are these high, middle, or low frequency words? What kinds of words have a frequency of over 1,000?

M34.   Bartlett, John. Familiar Quotations: A Collection of Passages, Phrases and Proverbs Traced to their Sources in Ancient and Modern Literature. 14th ed. rev. and enl.   Ed. Emily Morrison Beck. Boston: Little, Brown, 1968.

Bartlett's is the standard compendium, useful for locating the source of quotations and for verifying their wording. It is comprehensive, accurate, and conveniently arranged.   The work proper is ordered chronologically; the two indexes provide an author-subject (keyword) approach.

Contents:

1)   International in scope.
2)   From 3500 B.C. (ancient Egypt) to the late 1960's.
3)   Poetry and prose. [1]
4)   Anonymous quotations as well as those by known authors.
5)   For known authors, birth and death dates are given.

6) Works from which quotations are taken are dated.
7) Exact location of quotation is cited (chapter and verse; act, scene, and line; etc.).
8) For non-English quotations, the original wording is given in a footnote if the language is familiar.

Arrangement:

1) How to use Bartlett's, pp. xv–xviii.
2) Chronological entries.
3) Anonymous quotations arranged chronologically beginning p. 1083; see p. 149 ff. for anonymous Greek and Latin quotations prior to the thirteenth century.
4) Footnotes to entries: similar thoughts expressed by other writers, cross-references, history of sources, and other annotations.
5) Alphabetical index of authors with their dates, p. 1107ff.
6) Alphabetical index by keywords, p. 1155ff: unusually full; several keywords for each quotation.

Review Questions:

1) How extensive is Bartlett's coverage?

2) According to what principle are the main entries arranged?

3) According to what principle are the indexes arranged?

4) How do you use a keyword index?

Research Problems:

1) Identify the exact source of both quotations:
   a) "The almond tree shall flourish, and the grasshopper shall be a burden, and desire shall fail; because man goeth to his long home, and the mourners go about the streets..."
   b) "The stroke of death is as a lover's pinch, /Which hurts, and is desir'd."

2) What did Charles Lamb have to say about mountains? Edna St. Vincent Millay about burning the candle at both ends? Swift about satire? (Cite sources.)

3) What famous remarks have been attributed to Alexander the Great?

Notes (Bartlett's)

1. More complete coverage of British quotations, especially
    quotations from British poetry, can be found in The
    Oxford Dictionary of Quotations, 2nd ed. (n. p.:   Ox-
    ford University Press, 1955).
            Another useful work is Magill's Quotations in
    Context, ed. Frank N. Magill (New York: Harper &
    Row, 1965) and its supplementary Second Series (1969);
    Magill presents the quotation in a context of from ap-
    proximately seven to fifteen lines, provides a brief
    (about two hundred words) plot summary or description
    of the work in which the quotation appears, and ex-
    plains the relevance of the quotation to the larger con-
    text.
            Also see Brewer's Dictionary of Phrase and
    Fable (S11) and The Oxford Dictionary of English Prov-
    erbs (S14).

M35a.   The Library of Literary Criticism of English and
        American Authors. Ed. Charles Wells Moulton.
        8 vols. 1901 [-1905]; rpt. Gloucester, Mass.:
        Peter Smith, 1959.

M35b.   The Critical Temper: A Survey of Modern Criticism
        of English and American Literature from the Be-
        ginnings to the Twentieth Century. Ed. Martin
        Tucker. 3 vols. New York: Frederick Ungar,
        1969.

        These compilations of critical quotations are valuable
not only in themselves but also as an index to literary criticism. Works from which the extracts are taken are given
full bibliographical citations and thus are easy to locate.
Moulton's original work provides a convenient survey of nineteenth-century critical opinions about past and contemporary
literature.
        Moulton is described below in detail; significant dif-
ferences between Moulton and Tucker are noted under The
Critical Temper.

Contents (Moulton):

1) Extracts from selected critical writings (manuscripts,

journals, letters, articles, books, etc.) about English
and American authors.
2) Coverage of authors and their critics from 680 A.D.
to 1904. [1]
3) Brief biographical sketches of the authors.
4) Definitive editions and biography. [2]

Arrangement:

1) Table of Contents at the beginning of each volume arranged alphabetically by author. Authors' birth and
death dates given.
2) Table of engravings.
3) Main entries: arranged chronologically (i.e., Vol. I
covers the years 680 to 1618; it begins with <u>Beowulf</u>
and ends with Ben Jonson and Sir Robert Ayton).
4) Each main entry contains a biographical sketch, followed by personal criticism, criticism of individual
works, and general criticism; within the last three
categories, criticism is presented chronologically,
from contemporary to recent.
5) Exact source references cited.
6) Two indexes at end of Vol. III:
  a. index to authors, arranged alphabetically, giving
  volume, page, and birth and death dates.
  b. index to criticisms, arranged alphabetically by
  critic, specifying the author treated, volume, and
  page.

Contents and Arrangement (Critical Temper):

1) Twentieth-century criticism.
2) Only those authors covered by Moulton whose reputations are still commonly acknowledged.
3) Critical sub-sections arranged in this order:
  a. personal criticism.
  b. criticism of works in general.
  c. criticism of specific works.
4) Explanation of abbreviations of periodical titles cited
in the main entries: found at the beginning of each
volume.

Review Questions:

1) In which work can you find twentieth-century criticism
of pre-twentieth-century authors?

2) In which work can you find twentieth-century criticism of American authors?

3) Where are the indexes to Moulton and The Critical Temper? How are they arranged?

4) Aside from critical excerpts, what information can be found in Moulton?

5) Why is it useful to have critical excerpts entered chronologically?

Research Problems:

1) In The Critical Temper's biographical sketch of Byron, what information is given about the character of Byron's father, Byron's relationship with his half-sister, and the identity of Claire Clairmont? Can this information be found in Moulton? What caveat may be inferred regarding the use of nineteenth-century reference works?

2) At what schools did Longfellow teach? What did Edward Everett Hale think of him as a teacher? On the basis of Evangeline, where did Hawthorne place Longfellow as a poet? Is Longfellow's poetic achievement highly valued by modern critics?

3) Primarily for what quality was Beowulf praised in the nineteenth century? According to Klaeber, in what way is Beowulf more than a narrative of notable events? What modern critic discusses Beowulf's death as a reflection of God's foreknowledge and will? In what work?

Notes (Moulton)

1. Similar coverage of twentieth-century authors can be found in these important supplements to Moulton: A Library of Literary Criticism: Modern American Literature, ed. Dorothy Nyren Curley, Maurice Kramer, and Elaine Fialka Kramer, 4th enl. ed., 3 vols. (New York: Frederick Ungar, 1969); and A Library of Literary Criticism: Modern British Literature, ed. Ruth Z. Temple and Martin Tucker, 3 vols. (New York: Frederick Ungar, 1966).

Check your library's card catalog under the title A Library of Literary Criticism for works on modern German and romance literatures.

2. These are now chiefly of historical interest.

M36a. The New Encyclopaedia Britannica. 15th ed.   30
        vols. Chicago: Encyclopaedia Britannica, 1974.

M36b. Britannica Book of the Year [1938--].

       Britannica's fifteenth edition--Britannica 3 or The
New Encyclopaedia Britannica--derives its titles from its
new tripartite format. The one-volume Propaedia[1] is a topical table of contents, the nineteen-volume Macropaedia provides extensive studies, and the ten-volume Micropaedia
serves both as a source of capsule information and as an index to the Macropaedia. Thus, the format reflects the editors' attempt to provide: 1) a sense of a topic's place within
the framework of human knowledge, 2) an in-depth study of
the topic, and 3) a brief "ready reference" summary of that
topic.
       Generally, the user will begin by consulting the Micro-
paedia, where he will find a brief article on his subject, with
cross-references to further entries in the Micropaedia and/
or Macropaedia. Eventually, he may wish to refer to the
Propaedia's outline of knowledge to better understand his subject's place in the grand scheme of things. For the student
of literature, of course, Britannica will be most useful as
an introduction to extra-literary subjects. [2]
       Micropaedia articles will easily be kept up-to-date,
since the information upon which they are based is stored
in computers. [3] Further updating is provided by the Britannica Book of the Year, an ongoing publication. The 1974
volume of Britannica Book of the Year is described below
as an example of the yearbook's current format.

Contents and Arrangement (Propaedia):

1) How to Use the Propaedia, pp. 8-9.
2) Table of Contents (to the Propaedia only), pp. 10-16.
3) The outline proper divided into ten parts:
    a. matter and energy.
    b. the earth.
    c. life on earth.
    d. human life.
    e. human society.
    f. art.
    g. technology.

      h.   religion.
      i.   the history of mankind.
      j.   the branches of knowledge.

4) Authoritative introductory essays to each part; for example, Mark Van Doren introduces The World of Art. [4]
5) Further analytical breakdown into divisions and sections of learning, each preceded by an explanatory headnote.
6) Ultimate breakdown into separate subjects. Page references for each subject are given in three columns, from the broadest to the most specific. (Note that these page references are to the Macropaedia only.) [5]
7) Identification of authors of the Macropaedia articles, new pp. 7ff. at back: includes institutional affiliation and major publications.

Contents (Macropaedia):

1) Signed major articles on all subjects by authorities in their fields, e.g., Arnold Toynbee on Time, Antonia Frazer on Mary Queen of Scots, Arthur Mizener on F. Scott Fitzgerald.
2) Illustrations and maps in the text.
3) Classified and evaluative bibliographies appended to articles.

Arrangement:

1) Alphabetically arranged.
2) Many of the lengthier articles both introduced and outlined.
3) Both marginal subheadings and boldface subheadings within the text.

Contents (Micropaedia):

1) "Ready reference" articles of 750 words or less.
2) Synopses of Macropaedia major articles.
3) Numerous maps, illustrations, and statistical charts in the text.
4) Addenda: Statistical summaries and explanations of map legends and abbreviations.

Arrangement:

1) Alphabetically arranged.
2) Cross-references to other Micropaedia articles: indicated by see, see also, q.v., or RELATED ENTRIES.

3)   Cross-references to Macropaedia articles: indicated by Arabic numerals flanking a colon (2:340b). The first number denotes the volume, the second the page. The letter following the second number refers to the quarter of the two-column Macropaedia page cited, the page being thought of so:

                a   e
                b   f
                c   g
                d   h

4)   Cross-references to illustrations ("illus.") other than those in the major article.

5)   Table of Contents to Addenda, X, 910.

Contents and Arrangement (1974 Book of the Year):

1)   Table of Contents listing Feature Articles, "1973 Chronology of Major Events," and Special Reports.

2)   Other articles are generally short and are entered under specific headings, alphabetically arranged; these articles also cover the events of the preceding year. Of special interest to literature students are "Biography," "Literature," "Obituaries," "Theatre," and "Words and Meanings, New."

3)   Identification of contributors to this Book of the Year.

4)   Cumulative (but selective) index to articles and tables in this Book of the Year and the two previous ones.

Review Questions:

1)   Which parts of Britannica 3 are alphabetically arranged? Which one of these parts serves as an index? Why does this alphabetically arranged work require an index?

2)   Which part contains long articles? Which contains the topical table of contents or outline of knowledge? Which contains bibliographies?

3)   Where can you discover who wrote a particular article?

4)   Which are the famous older editions of Britannica?

5)   Where can you learn about Alan Bates? About the meaning of "judder"? Where can you learn how many books are in your college library and how this figure compares with that of other college libraries?

Research Problems:

Britannica, 15th and 11th editions

1) Whose folk beliefs were codified in the Malleus maleficarum? What is the English title of this work? Using the Propaedia, trace the relationship between the general topic of religion and folk beliefs concerning witchcraft by noting the appropriate analytical headings. Does the eleventh edition's discussion of the Malleus contain any surprising additional information about confessions of witchcraft extracted through torture?

Britannica Book of the Year 1974

2) Name the most important Yiddish work published in 1973. What is a "doomster"? What is "rebunk"? Name four popular historical biographies by Nancy Mitford (died 1973).

Britannica, 15th edition

3) Where is Culloden, and what are its associations with the Young Pretender? Whose grandson was the Young Pretender? How did the Forty-five Rebellion ultimately affect Highland Scotland?

Notes (Britannica)

1. Propaedia, Macropaedia, and Micropaedia are the editors' neologisms for before, great, and little learning.

2. The Columbia Encyclopedia, ed. William Bridgwater and Seymour Kurtz, 3rd ed. (New York: Columbia University Press, 1967) is an excellent one-volume general encyclopedia. "Intended for the use of specialists but only in the fields outside their specialty" (Preface), The Columbia Encyclopedia makes a useful scholarly addition to one's personal reference collection.
    For major extra-literary research, the student will want to consult such specialized encyclopedias as the International Encyclopedia of the Social Sciences (S87), The Encyclopedia of Philosophy (S88), Encyclopaedia of Religion and Ethics (S89), New Catholic Encyclopedia (S90), Encyclopedia Judaica (S91), Encyclopedia of World Art (S92), and Grove's Dictionary of

Music and Musicians (S93).   Also see the Dictionary
of the History of Ideas (S33).

3. If currency is not of the essence, the famous ninth (1875-
   89) and eleventh (1910-11) editions are of great value.
   Treatment of subjects in the humanities and history is
   frequently more detailed than in the latest edition, and
   among the contributors to these editions are writers
   who have themselves become subjects of research,
   e.g., Algernon Swinburne, William Morris, and Lord
   Macaulay.

4. Literature, as a particular art, occupies eight pages of
   Part VI.   Outlined are theoretical aspects of literature, literature's relationship to the other arts, technical aspects, literary types, popular literature, the
   history of literature, and national and folk literatures.
   There follows a list of biographical articles in the
   Macropaedia on literary figures.

5. Since the classifications are often arbitrary (and to sec-
   ond-guess the editors may be unduly time consuming),
   the Propaedia should be used as the final, not the
   initial, locating source to check on the comprehensiveness of Micropaedia cross-references.

        For explanation of the page reference designa-
   tion, see Micropaedia--Arrangement, #3.

Research Problems:

1) Compile a list of major Russian poets born after 1920.
   Which of these were once married to each other?

2) Who wrote Britannica's major article on Shakespeare?
   (Use the 15th edition.) Name the authors of the two
   standard multivolumed works on the theatre in Shakespeare's time. Where in Britannica is Caroline Spurgeon's analysis of Shakespeare's imagery discussed?
   What does Miss Spurgeon conclude about Shakespeare
   the man?

3) What is the "FitzGerald stanza"? Quote one. How did
   FitzGerald's best known work affect his era?

4) Give the history of the poem, the first stanza of which
   appears below:
   > Stay with me God. The night is dark,
   > The night is cold: my little spark
   > Of courage dies. The night is long;
   > Be with me, God, and make me strong.

5) What nineteenth-century English poet wrote a play about
   Mary Tudor, who preceded Elizabeth as Queen of England? What two other historical figures did he use as
   the subjects of plays?

6) Using a specialized serial bibliography, discover the
   thesis of Paul J. Korshin's "Johnson and Swift: A Study
   in the Genesis of Literary Opinion" (1969).

7) Is D. H. Lawrence the author of an essay entitled "State
   of Funk," written prior to 1931? In what collection does
   this essay appear? Cite author, title of book, publisher,
   and date.

8) Determine whether "air" is one of Yeats' characteristic
   words by noting in how many of his plays he uses some
   form of "air." Is this number more or less than half
   of the plays he wrote? (Count A and B texts as one
   play.)

9) Frank Lloyd Wright was ostensibly the inspiration for the hero of what American novel?

10) Cite two works (with their Winchell code numbers) in which you can find extensive bibliographies of science fiction or fantasy subjects.

11) List four collections of the letters of the poet William Morris (1834-96).

12) Compile a list of articles on Chaucer's "Merchant's Tale" abstracted in AES during 1962 and 1963. (Cite full bibliographical information for each.)

13) How was Spenser's poetry regarded by the sixteenth-century scholar William Camden? What did Dr. Johnson think of the stanzaic form of the Faerie Queene? In which of his poems does Keats allude to the Faerie Queene?

14) How did American writers support themselves between World Wars I and II? Name the literary historian whom you are following.

15) What childhood incident made George Bernard Shaw aware that his father was an irresponsible drinker? Who is the biographer you are following?

16) In what work can you find a listing of Arthur Miller's short stories, radio plays, essays, and interviews? What other information does this work contain? Name the first full-length study of Norman Mailer. Cite an article by James Baldwin on Norman Mailer.

17) When was Richard Henry Dana Jr.'s An Autobiographical Sketch (1815-1842) first published in its entirety? How large was the edition? Where can a copy be seen?

18) Quote the epigraph Yeats wrote to Cathleen ni Houlihan. In which edition can it be found? In his letter to Lady Gregory (February, 1903), what incident does Yeats recount as the inspiration for this play?

19) Prepare a list of works published in 1969 about the twentieth-century American writer Kurt Vonnegut. (Explain all abbreviations.)

20) What films did Franco Zeffirelli make in the 1960's? For what is he famous aside from filmmaking? Where does he live?

21) Cite three anthologies containing seventeenth-century French dramas translated into English.

22) Cite an example from a Shakespearean tragedy of an "exciting force."

23) Cite two bibliographies of Increase Mather. Give full bibliographical information including number of entries and number of copies printed.

24) What is "metatheatre"? Name two plays by Jean Genet that are considered examples of metatheatre. Cite three critical works concerned with metatheatre.

25) What is the focus of a magazine entitled Stereo Head-phones? How many languages are included in the text? Explain all items of information concerning the journal in the order in which they are presented in your source.

26) What work of the modern author Syed Waliullah is best known outside India? What is it about? Where can one find reviews of Waliullah's work?

27) Who published the most inexpensive unabridged edition of Sons and Lovers available in 1974? (Ignore discounted prices.)

28) Which modern German poet did the British scholar J. B. Leishman translate and edit in 1964? Cite the title of Leishman's work. How long did major reviewers show interest in this work? With what critical work did Leishman follow this edition/translation?

29) Cite two explicatory criticisms of Milton's "On the Late Massacre in Piedmont."

30) The second edition of Gita May's Diderot et Baudelaire, critiques d'art was published in 1967. In what year does the Bibliographic Index first cite the second edition? Is the bibliography May includes primary, secondary, or both? How many pages long is it? Is it annotated?

31) Compile a list of renderings into modern English of Sir

Gawain and the Green Knight published through 1900.
Cite only rare editions, excluding post-1900 reprints.
Which one of these is held by the Library of Congress?

32) Cite the author and title of a burlesque on Mary Woll-
stonecraft, published in Boston in 1795.   Who else is
satirized in this work?

33) Who is the author of a dissertation that is actually a
critical edition of Lyly's Mother Bombie?   Which text
of the play is considered authoritative?   Where in the
dissertation is the play interpreted?   What values are
expressed through Lyly's use of antithetical structure?

34) Who printed the first 1616 edition of Chapman's translation of Homer?   What was its original title?   What
British libraries and collectors hold copies of the original edition?

35) What was the Eleutheria?   Name six classical writers
who serve as a source for relevant information.

36) Note the sixteenth-century meanings of the adjective
"tall" which differ from its twentieth-century meanings.

CHAPTER VI

ANNOTATED LIST OF SUPPLEMENTARY WORKS*

DICTIONARIES, LITERARY ENCYCLOPEDIAS,
HANDBOOKS, AND GUIDES

Literature: British and American

S1.   Halkett, Samuel, and John Laing. Dictionary of Anon-
       ymous and Pseudonymous Literature. New and
       enlarged edition by James Kennedy, W. A. Smith,
       and A. F. Johnson. 9 vols. [Vols. VIII (1900-
       1950) and IX (Additions and Corrections) by Dennis
       E. Rhodes and Anna E. C. Simoni.] Edinburgh:
       Oliver and Boyd, 1926-62.
       Halkett and Laing's work, which first appeared in 1882,
and has been regularly updated, is still considered the best
source for identifying the authors of anonymous and pseudo-
nymous English literature. Arranged alphabetically by the
first word of the title (other than "A," "An," "The"), the
dictionary notes the format and pagination of the first edition,
the number of volumes, the place and date of publication, the
name of its author, and the source for attribution of authorship. Coverage extends through 1949, and includes literary
works in English printed abroad and literary works translated
into English.
       Volume I contains a list of authorities cited for attri-
bution of authorship. The first supplement is found at the
back of Volume VI. Two indexes (the first to authors, the
second to initials and pseudonyms) appear in Volume VII.
Volume VIII contains additions from 1900 through 1949, and
Volume IX is composed of additions and corrections to all
the earlier volumes. Both Volumes VIII and IX have their
own indexes.

_____
*Asterisks denote works that are universally valuable.

For other works that attribute authorship, see M23, note 3.

*S2.   Wright, Andrew. A Reader's Guide to English and American Literature. Glenview, Ill.: Scott, Foresman, 1970.
A list of "the most reliable editions of the principal authors and the best works of biography and criticism" (Preface). Reference works on English, American, and foreign literatures are also included. Index of authors at back. A useful and inexpensive paperback.

S3.   Bateson, F. W. A Guide to English Literature. Rev. ed. Chicago: Aldine Publishing, 1968.
A guide to authoritative editions, major criticism, reliable biographies, and literary background of principal British authors by the editor of the CBEL (M5, n. 2). Short critical essays and articles are for the most part excluded. Coverage generally extends through 1966. Bateson's arrangement is chronological by literary period and, within the period, chronological by birthdate of the author. Special chapters are devoted to general works on English literature, literary criticism in English, and literary scholarship. Interchapters between bibliographies are historio-critical essays on the major literary periods. Index at back.

S4.   The New Century Handbook of English Literature. Ed. Clarence L. Barnhart. Rev. ed. New York: Appleton, 1967.
The New Century Handbook covers essentially the same material as the OCEL (M1); however, the former is intended specifically for the American (rather than English) reader in need of more assistance with British and continental history, geography, and pronunciation. Coverage of recent English authors and of literary terms and movements is more extensive than the OCEL's.

S5.   The Penguin Companion to English Literature. Ed. David Daiches. New York: McGraw-Hill, 1971.
Mostly biographical entries; see Penguin Companion to Literature; European (M12) for format. Select List of Bibliographical, Historical, and Background Works, pp. 573-[576].

S6.   The Reader's Encyclopedia of Shakespeare. Ed. Oscar James Campbell and Edward G. Quinn. New York: Thomas Y. Crowell, 1966.
Covers all facets of Shakespeare's life, theatre,

reputation, and works. Under entries for individual plays,
probable sources and dates of composition, plot summaries,
major criticisms, and production histories are provided.
The appendices include a chronological outline of Shakespeare's life and works, transcripts of documents relating
to Shakespeare, and a thirty-page classified bibliography.
Alphabetically arranged; illustrated.

S7.   Temple, Ruth Z., and Martin Tucker, eds. Twentieth
          Century British Literature: A Reference Guide
          and Bibliography. New York: Frederick Ungar,
          1968.
          Part I is an annotated reference guide to books about
twentieth-century British literature. Noted in the Table of
Contents are such categories as bibliographies of bibliographies, sources for biography, journals, histories, essays,
and criticism (subdivided by genre). Part II consists of bibliographies of some four hundred authors and is an updated
and expanded version of Temple and Tucker's A Library of
Literary Criticism: Modern British Literature (M35, note
1). Alphabetically arranged by author, Part II lists the author's works, their genres and publication dates, and reference sources about the author. A list of authors included is
found on pp. 119-25. An Index of Authors appears at the
back.

S8.   Burke, W. J., and Will D. Howe. American Authors
          and Books 1640 to the Present Day. 3rd rev. ed.
          Rev. by Irving Weiss and Anne Weiss. New York:
          Crown Publishers, 1972.
          Brief dictionary entries for authors with selected list
of works and their dates. Short descriptions under title entries. A few subject entries, e.g., Hippies, Brook Farm,
Little Magazines. Includes more minor writers and more
recent ones than does the OCAL (M2).

S9.   Herzberg, Max J., et al. The Reader's Encyclopedia
          of American Literature. New York: Thomas Y.
          Crowell, 1962.
          Similar to the OCAL (M2). Glossary of Literary
Terms at back.

S10.   Jones, Howard Mumford, and Richard M. Ludwig.
          Guide to American Literature and its Backgrounds
          since 1890. 4th ed., rev. and enl. Cambridge,
          Mass.: Harvard University Press, 1972.
          A bibliographical outline including excellent headnote

introductions to various aspects of the period covered. Jones
and Ludwig present "in understandable order the combination
of intellectual and sociological (political) event and literary
productivity, which is at once the peril and the exhilaration
of this enterprise" (General Introduction). Table of Contents
and publishers' abbreviations at front. Index of primary and
secondary authors at back.

Literature: General and World

S11. Brewer's Dictionary of Phrase and Fable. Centenary
          Edition. Rev. by Ivor H. Evans. London: Cas-
          sell, 1970.
        An updated nineteenth-century work described on the
title page of earlier editions as "giving the derivation, source,
or origin of common phrases, allusions, and words that have
a tale to tell." Phrases are colloquial or proverbial; allusions are historical, literary, mythological, biblical, etc.
Alphabetically arranged. Both a reference tool and a brows-
er's delight.

S12. Funk and Wagnalls Standard Dictionary of Folklore,
          Mythology and Legend. Ed. Maria Leach and
          Jerome Fried. 2 vols. 1949-50; rpt. in 1 vol.
          with minor corrections. New York: F&W, 1972.
        Representative but worldwide coverage of gods, he-
roes, nature lore and legends, folk dances and songs, festivals, rituals, childrens' games, magic, folklore scholars,
etc. Some extensive signed scholarly articles with bibliographies. Greek mythology is de-emphasized. Alphabetically
arranged.

S13. Thompson, Stith. Motif-Index of Folk Literature.
          Rev. and enl. ed. 6 vols. Bloomington: In-
          diana University Press, 1955-58.
        Subtitled "a classification of narrative elements in
folktales, ballads, myths, fables, mediaeval romances, ex-
empla, fabliaux, jest-books and local legends," the Motif-
Index logically arranges these elements according to a numerical system and locates information about them by page
references to standard folklore studies. To use this work
fully and accurately, the student must read the Introduction.

S14. The Oxford Dictionary of English Proverbs. 3rd ed.
          Rev. by F. P. Wilson. Oxford: Clarendon Press,
          1970.

Alphabetically arranged by significant words with cross-references. Earliest literary reference and some later references are cited.

S15.   Benét, William Rose. The Reader's Encyclopedia.
            2nd ed. New York: Thomas Y. Crowell, 1965.
        Treatment similar to the OCEL (M1), but covers all
literatures. Alphabetically arranged; illustrated.

*S16.   Cassell's Encyclopaedia of World Literature. Ed.
            J. Buchanan-Brown. [2nd ed.] Rev. and enl.
            3 vols. London: Cassell, 1973.
        Though brief, articles are signed, and bibliographies
are appended to all biographies and to many other entries.
Volume I contains histories of individual literatures, literary
terms, genres, schools, movements, themes, and topics
(including influential literary works). Volumes II and III
are devoted to author biographies (with selected primary and
secondary bibliographies) and to anonymous works; author
and title entries arranged in a single alphabet. Credentials
of contributors at front of Volume I. Contributors' initials,
Key to Special Signs, and Notes for the User at front of each
volume.

S17.   Encyclopedia of World Literature in the 20th Century.
            Ed. Wolfgang Bernard Fleischmann. 3 vols. New
            York: Frederick Ungar, 1967.
        Similar to the Penguin Companion series (M12) but
limited to the twentieth century. Short signed articles of a
biographical and critical nature. Primary and secondary
bibliographies. Alphabetically arranged; plates.

S18.   The Oxford Companion to the Theatre. Ed. Phyllis
            Hartnoll. 3rd ed. London: Oxford University
            Press, 1967.
        Miss Hartnoll takes all drama for her province. Em-
phasis is upon plays in performance. Motion pictures are
excluded. Appended are a forty-five page classified bibliography of theatre books and 176 annotated illustrations.

S19.   The Reader's Encyclopedia of World Drama. Ed.
            John Gassner and Edward Quinn. New York:
            Thomas Y. Crowell, 1969.
        Unlike Phyllis Hartnoll's Oxford Companion to the
Theatre (S18), which emphasizes popular drama and production aspects, The Reader's Encyclopedia of World Drama is
concerned with drama as literature. There are no entries

for actors, acting companies, theaters, etc. A valuable inclusion is the appended Basic Documents in Dramatic Theory.
Alphabetically arranged; illustrated.

S20.   Kienzle, Siegfried. Modern World Theater: A Guide
          to Productions in Europe and the United States
          since 1945. Trans. Alexander and Elizabeth
          Henderson. New York: Frederick Ungar, 1970.
       The most recent reference work on post-World War
II drama. Extensive plot summaries. Arranged alphabetically by author. Index of play titles at end.

*S21. Encyclopedia of Poetry and Poetics. Ed. Alex Prem-
          inger, Frank J. Warke, and O. B. Hardison, Jr.
          Princeton: Princeton University Press, 1965.
          [New title: Princeton Encyclopedia of Poetry and
          Poetics.]
       Signed, highly specialized articles on poetic terms,
schools, critical theory, etc. Brief bibliographies appended
to articles. No entries for individual poets or poems.

*S22. The New Oxford Annotated Bible with the Apocrypha.
          Ed. Herbert G. May and Bruce M. Metzgar.
          New York: Oxford University Press, 1973.
       "An Ecumenical Study Bible" based on the Revised
Standard Version and containing the second edition of the New
Testament. Includes "Introductions, Comments, Cross-References, General Articles, Measures and Weights, Chronological Tables of Rulers, Maps, and Indexes." Annotations
and articles by eminent biblical scholars. Particularly useful to students of literature are such articles as "Characteristics of Hebrew Poetry" and "Literary Forms in the Gos-
pels." Table of Contents, p. v; indexes to annotations and
maps at back.

S23.   The Interpreter's Dictionary of the Bible. 4 vols.
          New York: Abingdon, 1962.
       Subtitled "an illustrated encyclopedia identifying and
explaining all proper names and significant terms and subjects in the Holy Scriptures, including the Apocrypha with
attention to archaeological discoveries and researches into
the life and faith of ancient times." References are to the
Revised Standard Version of the Bible. Signed articles by
recognized scholars; bibliographies. Alphabetically arranged.

S24.   The New Century Classical Handbook. Ed. Catherine
          A. Avery. New York: Appleton, 1962.

Unlike The Oxford Classical Dictionary (M11), this
handbook is aimed at the general reader and student: bibliographies and exact reference citations are omitted; plot summaries, a pronunciation guide, drawings, photographs, and
maps are included. Coverage extends only through 68 A.D.

S25.   The Oxford Companion to Classical Literature. Ed.
        Sir Paul Harvey. 1937; rpt. Oxford: Clarendon
        Press, 1966.
        The OCCL deals not only with Greek and Roman lit-
eratures but also with connections between these and medieval
and modern English literature. Entries for authors, titles,
forms, allusions, persons, and background relevant to the
study of classical literature. List of General Articles, pronunciation guide, and abbreviations at front. Date Chart of
Classical Literature, Table of Weights and Measures, descriptions of plates, the plates themselves, and maps at back.

S26.   Graves, Robert. The Greek Myths. 2 vols. Balti-
        more: Penguin Books, 1955.
        A complete recounting of the myths by an eminent
poet, historical novelist, and scholar. Graves presents variant elements of each myth, cites classical sources, and offers anthropological and archaeological interpretation. Map
at the front of Volume I and on the back endpaper of Volume
II. Each volume has its own table of contents. Index to
both volumes at the back of Volume II.

S27.   The Oxford Companion to French Literature. Ed.
        Sir Paul Harvey and J. E. Heseltine. 1959;
        rpt. Oxford: Clarendon Press, 1961.
        Similar in contents and arrangement to the OCEL
(M1), this is a pre-World War II survey, containing a useful
appended bibliography for beginning students of French literature and culture. Maps at back.

Language and Usage

*S28.   The American Heritage Dictionary of the English Lan-
        guage. Ed. William Morris. Boston: American
        Heritage Publishing and Houghton Mifflin, 1969.
        An excellent one-volume modern dictionary. Not only
records the language but also suggests precise usage (both
British and American). Inclusion of slang and vulgar words.
Readable entries: minimal use of abbreviation; no training
in phonetics necessary for pronunciation. Profusely illus-

trated; many photographs. Essays on language by noted
scholars (see Table of Contents).

S29. Webster's New Dictionary of Synonyms. Springfield,
      Mass.: G. &C. Merriam, 1968.
      Subtitled "a dictionary of discriminated synonyms with
antonyms and analogous and contrasted words, " Webster's is
both more comprehensive and simpler to use than Roget's
classic Thesaurus (1852), the latter actually intended for a
different purpose--discovering a specific word, having begun
with a general concept. See Explanatory Notes [p. 32a] for
analysis of entries. A particularly helpful feature of this dictionary is the citing of quotations from literature to discrimi-
nate synonyms through a context. A list of authors quoted, with
dates and professional specialization, appears at the end.

*S30. Nicholson, Margaret. A Dictionary of American-
       English Usage. New York: Oxford University
       Press, 1957.
      Based on the first edition of Fowler's Modern English
Usage, this is an indispensable guide to accurate diction.
Presents correct idiomatic prepositions, precise differences
between similar words, preferred spellings, plurals, pronun-
ciations, "vague" words to avoid, etc.

S31. Bernstein, Theodore M. The Careful Writer: A
      Modern Guide to English Usage. New York:
      Atheneum, 1965.
      While not as exhaustive as Nicholson's work (S30),
The Careful Writer covers much the same ground. Bern-
stein, a New York Times editor, amuses as he enlightens.
Witness his entry for "fine": "As an adverb, fine is classi-
fied by Webster as dialectal and colloquial. So if you write,
'He is behaving fine, ' you are not writing good. "

*S32. The MLA Style Sheet. 2nd ed. New York: Modern
       Language Association of America, 1970.
      A manual of stylistic conventions widely accepted by
editors of scholarly journals and university presses. MLA
Style Sheet form, with various modifications, is prescribed
by most graduate schools for M.A. theses and doctoral dissertations. Discussed here are such matters as the use of
quotations, italics, numerals, capitals, foreign abbreviations,
documentation, etc. No "sheet" but a full-length book is A Manual of Style: For Authors, Editors, and Copywriters, 12th ed.,
rev. (Chicago: University of Chicago Press, 1969), for those
writing for publication.

Extra-literary

S33. Dictionary of the History of Ideas: Studies of Selected
      Pivotal Ideas. Ed. Philip P. Wiener. 4 vols.
      New York: Scribner, 1973.
      Lengthy signed articles by internationally known schol-
ars. The studies, necessarily selective, are of three kinds:
"cross-cultural studies limited to a given century or period,
studies that trace an idea from antiquity to later periods,
and studies that explicate the meaning of a pervasive idea
and its development in the minds of its leading proponents"
(Preface). An extensive bibliography follows each article.
Cross-references in brackets following bibliography; the most
significant references are printed in boldface. An Analytical
Table of Contents for all four volumes is found at the front
of Volume I. There follows a List of Articles, alphabetically
arranged, and a List of Contributors with institutional affiliation and publications.

S34. Steinberg's Dictionary of British History. Ed. S. H.
      Steinberg and I. H. Evans. London: Edward
      Arnold, 1970.
      Alphabetically arranged handbook of "political, consti-
tutional, administrative, legal, ecclesiastical, and economic
events" (Preface). No purely biographical entries.

S35. Walford, A. J. Guide to Reference Material. 2nd
      ed. 3 vols. London: Library Association,
      1966-70.
      British publication somewhat more comprehensive
than Winchell (M13), particularly in regard to British and
European reference works. Annotations are often fuller,
too. Contents:
Volume I.   Science and Technology.
Volume II.   Social and Historical Sciences, Philosophy and
             Religion.
Volume III. Generalia, Language and Literature, The Arts.
Each volume has its own index.

BIOGRAPHIES

British and American

S36. Who Was Who. 3rd ed. London: Adam and Charles
      Black, New York: St. Martin's, 1967.

Here are found the Who's Who entries for those no longer living. Volume I contains the biographies of people who died during the period 1897-1915; Volume II, 1916-1928; Volume III, 1929-1940; Volume IV, 1941-1950; Volume V, 1951-1960; Volume VI, 1961-1970. Further volumes will continue to appear at the close of each decade. Entries are alphabetically arranged within each volume.

S37. Dictionary of American Biography. Ed. Allen Johnson and Dumas Malone. 22 vols. 1928-58; rpt. in 11 vols. New York: Scribner's, 1958-64.

This American version of the DNB (M14) lists notable deceased Americans from all walks of life. Errata to the entire work are printed at the beginning of Volume I. Contributors are identified at the beginning of each volume. Arrangement is alphabetical, with bracketed bibliographies appended to each article. Volume X contains six separate indexes to Volumes I-IX: by subjects, contributors, birthplaces, schools and colleges, occupations, and topics. Volume XI contains two supplements: the first updates through 1935, the second through 1940.

S38. Who's Who in America 1972-1973. 37th ed. 2 vols. Chicago: Marquis Who's Who, 1972.

This American work records information similar to that of its British counterpart (M15). Standards of admission are exacting. Some international notables are included. Works and dates are cited for authors, composers, etc. Addenda appears at the end of Volume II. Note that Who's Who in America is a valuable tool for updating the Dictionary of American Biography (S37). A supplementary volume, Who's Who in America/Index by Professions is imminent.

S39. Who Was Who in America. 5 vols. plus Historical Volume. Chicago: Marquis Who's Who, 1943--.

Volumes I-IV are companion volumes to Who's Who in America (S38). In Volume I are entered alphabetically the biographies of those who died during the period 1897-1942; Volume II, 1943-1950; Volume III, 1951-1960; Volume IV, 1961-1968; Volume V, 1969-1973. The Historical Volume contains brief biographical sketches of notable Americans who died between 1607 and 1896 as well as biographical maps, historical charts, etc. An index to all six volumes appears at the end of Volume V. Who Was Who in America is a continuing work.

International

S40. Biography Index: A Cumulative Index to Biographical
          Material in Books and Magazines [1946]. New
          York: H. W. Wilson, 1947--.
          Quarterly issues with annual and triennial cumulations.
Indexes books, periodicals, and New York Times obituaries.
Biography is interpreted broadly to include not only pure biography but also autobiography, letters, diaries, memoirs,
journals, genealogies, bibliographies, and "creative" biographical works, i. e., plays, novels, etc. Biography Index
is arranged in two parts: 1) by name of the biographee,
and 2) by profession and occupation, authors being subdivided by nationality.

*S41. Chambers's Biographical Dictionary. Ed. J. O.
          Thorne. Rev. ed. New York: St. Martin's,
          1969.
          A one-volume international dictionary featuring read-
able articles and coverage from earliest times to the present. (Contemporary figures are well represented.) Chambers's cites standard full-length biographies and notes an author's more important works. Pronunciation of difficult
names is indicated. The subject index at the end of the
volume is a useful feature.

BIBLIOGRAPHIES

Bibliographies of Bibliographies

S42. Howard-Hill, Trevor Howard. Bibliography of British
          Literary Bibliographies. Oxford: Clarendon
          Press, 1969. (Volume I of a projected three-
          volume series entitled Index to British Literary
          Bibliography.)
          Indexes bibliographies and textual notes published as
books, as parts of books, or in periodicals, written in English and published in the English-speaking Commonwealth or
the United States after 1890. Covers all of British literature, printing, and publishing from its beginnings. Detailed
Table of Contents with categories for general, period, and

regional bibliographies; for types of books; subjects; and literary authors. (Shakespeare is excluded, being the sole
subject of Volume II, Shakespearean Bibliography and Textual
Criticism, 1971.) Index at back of contributing scholars,
subjects (including literary authors), and a few titles of anonymous works, journals, and basic reference tools.

S43.   Nilon, Charles H.   Bibliography of Bibliographies in
            American Literature. New York: R. R. Bowker,
            1970.
        Goes beyond Besterman (M17) and standard reference
works on American literature, book publishing, and American
history. Includes bibliographies, whether published separately or appearing as journal articles or parts of books. Divided into four main sections. Section I--Bibliography--in-
cludes Basic American Bibliographies (arranged chronologically by historical period covered), Library of Congress and
National Union Catalogs (arranged chronologically within topical areas), Other Basic Bibliographies, and General Bibliographies (these last two sub-sections and all following sub-
sections arranged alphabetically by authors' names). Section
II--Authors--is subdivided by centuries. Section III--Genre
--includes Literary History and Criticism, Drama, Fiction,
and Poetry. Section IV--Ancillary--is a miscellaneous category containing such entries as Cinema, Foreign Criticism
of American Literature, The Negro, Themes and Types, etc.
No cross-references. Author, title, and subject index at
back.

Current Bibliographies: British and American

S44.   Annual Bibliography of English Language and Litera-
            ture. Modern Humanities Research Association,
            1921--.
        A British publication, the "MHRA Bibliography" cor-
responds to the MLA International Bibliography (M7). American critical works are listed. So too are reviews in scholarly periodicals of secondary works on literature--a useful
inclusion not found in the MLA International Bibliography.
Index, "Authors and Subjects Treated," at back of each volume.

S45.   The Year's Work in English Studies [1919-20]. Pub-
            lished for the English Association. London: Ox-
            ford University Press [later John Murray], 1921--.

An annual, selective critical survey consisting of extensive bibliographical essays. Coverage includes the best
scholarly books, articles, and notes by English and American
critics on English literature and language. American literature is treated more briefly. Table of Contents for each
volume. Indexes to secondary authors, literary authors, and
subjects at back.

S46.   Bell, Inglis F., and Donald Baird. The English Novel
        1578-1956: A Checklist of Twentieth-Century Crit-
        icisms. Denver: Alan Swallow, 1958.
        Twentieth-century criticisms in English of English nov-
els from John Lyly's Euphues (1578) through novels of the
mid-1950's. Alphabetically arranged by author; within the
author entry by title. Masterlist of books and periodicals
cited at end (pp. 143ff). Introductory essay on the critical
status of the English novel at front.

        Temple, Ruth Z., and Martin Tucker, eds. Twentieth
        Century British Literature: A Reference Guide
        and Bibliography. (See S7.)

S47.   Gohdes, Clarence. Bibliographical Guide to the Study
        of Literature of the U.S.A. 3rd ed., rev. and
        enl. Durham, N.C.: Duke University Press,
        1970.
        An important selective, annotated bibliography, cover-
ing all genres and periods as well as many subjects related
to American literature, e.g., Philosophy and Psychology in
the United States, Religion, Arts Other Than Literature. Initial chapters are devoted to general reference tools and research techniques. Table of Contents and two indexes: Index
of Subjects and Index of Authors, Editors, and Compilers.
References are to numbered entries.

S48.   American Literary Scholarship: An Annual. Ed. Al-
        bert Robbins. Durham, N.C.: Duke University
        Press, 1965--.
        Annual, evaluative bibliographical essays by well-known
scholars surveying significant contributions (books as well as
articles) to American literature. Begins with criticism written in 1963. Table of Contents classifies by authors, period,
and genre. Key to abbreviations at front. Currently, an index of primary authors and contributing critics at back. Originally edited by James Woodress and sometimes still referred
to by his name.

S49a.   Leary, Lewis. Articles on American Literature 1900-

1950.   Durham, N. C.: Duke University Press,
1954.

S49b.   . Articles on American Literature 1950-
1967. Durham, N. C.: Duke University Press,
1970.
A selective but extensive listing of mostly English
language articles on American literature. Leary cumulates
articles entered in American Literature's quarterly checklists (M19a), in the MLA International Bibliography and its
antecedents (M7), and in a number of other sources (see his
Introductions for bibliographical sources and periodicals examined). The Table of Contents must be used for all but
author entries. Author listings arranged alphabetically by
critic. Subject entries arranged alphabetically by critic. Unannotated.

S50.   Eight American Authors: A Review of Research and
Criticism. Ed. James Woodress. Rev. ed. New
York: W. W. Norton, 1971.
Based on the 1956 edition by Floyd Stovall, Eight
American Authors is an excellent collection of bibliographical
essays on all aspects of scholarship and criticism relating to
Poe, Emerson, Hawthorne, Thoreau, Melville, Whitman,
Twain, and James. Five of the original contributors have
updated their essays; the other three are specialists in Mel-
ville, Whitman, and James respectively. Also see the com-
panion volume, Sixteen Modern [twentieth-century] American
Authors: A Survey of Research and Criticism, ed. Jackson
R. Bryer, rev. ed. (Durham, N. C.: Duke University Press,
1973).

Jones, Howard Mumford, and Richard M. Ludwig.
Guide to American Literature and its Backgrounds
since 1890. (See S10.)

S51.   Gerstenberger, Donna, and George Hendrick. The
American Novel, 1789-1959: A Checklist of
Twentieth-Century Criticism. Denver: Alan
Swallow, 1961. Supplemented by Vol. II, Criticism Written 1960-1968. Denver, 1970.
The first section of each volume contains criticism
of individual authors, arranged alphabetically; within the alphabetical listing, subdivided into individual novels, general
studies, and bibliographies. The second section lists criticism of the American novel as a genre and, after a general
section, is arranged chronologically by century. A master
list at the end of each volume provides complete bibliographical entries.

S52. British Museum. General Catalogue of Printed Books:
         Photolithographic Edition to 1955. 263 vols. Lon-
         don: Trustees of the British Museum, 1965.
      This is a cumulated reproduction of the first British
Museum Catalogue (1787) and its additions. Note that it is
not a union catalog but rather a record of all printed books
held by the national library of England from the fifteenth century through 1955, in all but the Oriental languages. (Like
the Library of Congress, the British Museum has been
awarded the copyright privilege.) It is essentially an author
catalog; however, some title and subject entries are included,
notably for biographies, which are entered under the name
of the biographee. Cross-references to anonyma, editors,
translators, etc. are extensive.
      The British Museum General Catalogue is continued
by its Ten Year Supplement 1956-1965, 50 vols. (London:
Trustees of the British Museum, 1968). Here, asterisked
entries with volume and page citations refer to entries in
the Catalogue to 1955 that have been corrected. Continuing
ten year supplements are projected.

S53. U. S. Library of Congress. A Catalog of Books Rep-
         resented by Library of Congress Printed Cards,
         Issued to July 31, 1942. 167 vols. Ann Arbor:
         Edwards Bros., 1942-46. (The "LC Catalog.")
      Prior to the printing of this catalog in 1942, the only
record of Library of Congress holdings consisted of a card
file at the Library of Congress itself, copies of which were
deposited in a number of large research libraries throughout
America. The "LC Catalog" was compiled to make this
record more accessible--a record more comprehensive than
that of any other single American library, since the Library
of Congress is legally entitled to receive all books copy-
righted in the United States and since its holdings of foreign
works are also most extensive. The catalog is a reprinting
of cards for books received by July 31, 1942. (It includes,
in addition, some books held by the Library of Congress for
which cards had not been printed as well as some cards for
books in other American libraries but not in the Library of
Congress.)
      The amount of information on the card may differ,
depending on the time of printing. More recent cards cite
author and dates, full title, edition, place and date of publication, number of copies printed if a small edition, pagination, special features (e. g., maps, bibliography), size, series, its LC subject classification, its LC number, and copyright number. The contents, especially of composite works
and periodicals, are often analyzed at length.

The "LC Catalog" is arranged alphabetically by author and anonymous title in a single alphabet. (If the author of an anonymous work has been supplied, the main entry will appear under his name, with a cross-reference from the title entry.) Complete works precede individual works. Card entries are explained only in Volume I.

S54.   Library of Congress and National Union Catalog Author Lists, 1942-1962: A Master Cumulation. 152 vols. Detroit: Gale Research, 1969-70.
A cumulation of the four Supplements to the "LC Catalog" and NUC issued between 1942 and 1962. From 1956 on, Gale becomes a union catalog. If no location is shown for a title represented by a printed LC card, the work is held by the Library of Congress. A Key to Location Symbols is found on the endpapers of each volume. Gale includes more title entries (for works likely to be known by title) than appear in the LC Supplements, thus simplifying the search. Works are listed generally in accordance with "LC Catalog" entry style. Explanation of the entry style appears at the front of each volume. If your library lacks this master cumulation, see the Supplements upon which it is based: Supplement: Cards Issued August 1, 1942-December 31, 1947 in 42 vols.
The Library of Congress Author Catalog [1948-52] in 24 vols.
The National Union Catalog: A Cumulative Author List 1953-57 in 28 vols. (Actually, a union catalog only for 1956-57; therefore, whether or not you use Gale, for a union catalog covering the years 1952-55, consult the following work, retrospectively produced:
National Union Catalog: 1952-1955 Imprints: An Author List in 30 vols. Finally, for the ongoing continuations of the NUC, consult The
National Union Catalog: A Cumulative Author List, [1956--] (M23b).

S55.   U.S. Library of Congress. The Library of Congress Catalog--Books: Subjects. Washington: Library of Congress, 1950--.
An alphabetically arranged listing by subject heading. For LC classifications, see the latest edition of Subject Headings Used in the Dictionary Catalogs of the Library of Congress and its supplements. Note such broad headings as Fiction in English (which includes all individual works of fiction or collections of works of fiction written in English by a single author) or Fiction in English--Translations. Many subheadings and cross-references to related headings are employed; the same work may be entered under several

headings. See the Guide to Use at the front of the first volume of each cumulation.

Almost all entries are located in at least one American library; the NUC supplies additional locations. Included
are entries for books, pamphlets, periodicals, and other
serials, in all languages, with imprint dates of 1945 or later,
which have been catalogued from 1950 on. Entries are ab-
breviated versions of "LC Catalog" cards. This subject listing is issued quarterly with annual and quinquennial cumulations.

Current Bibliographies: World

S56.   Cumulative Book Index: A World List of Books in the
        English Language. Minneapolis, later New York:
        H. W. Wilson, 1898--.
        As its subtitle indicates, the CBI goes beyond a na-
tional bibliography in its scope. Presently excluding little
more than federal government documents, music scores, and
ephemera, herein are catalogued all English language books
published since 1898. Since 1902 CBI has been arranged in
a single alphabetical order of authors, subjects, and titles.
Bibliographical information includes author or editor, title,
series, volume number if a multi-volumed work, edition,
pagination, binding (hardback or paper), price, and publisher.
Standard Book Number (i. e., purchase number) and LC card
number are cited when available. Author entries, located
through cross-references, are most extensive. Publishers'
addresses are listed at the back of each issue. CBI is currently published eleven times a year and cumulated annually.
Its permanent cumulations become supplements to the United
States Catalogue (M25, n. 2), thus forming the most comprehensive record of American book publishing from 1898 on.
        It should be pointed out that the CBI is a more com-
prehensive and multi-purposed tool than Books in Print
(M30a), though the latter's ubiquity has earned it a more detailed treatment in this guide.

S57.   Baldensperger, Fernand, and Werner P. Friederich.
        Bibliography of Comparative Literature. 1950;
        rpt. New York: Russell & Russell, 1960.
        A monumental listing arranged in four parts. Book
I deals with the theory of comparative literature; with inter-
mediaries between one literature and another; and with common themes, subjects, and genres. Book II covers the Ori-
ent and Antiquity, both generally and with respect to indi-

vidual authors. Book III, Aspects of Western Culture, traces broad literary and social influences from the end of the classical period to modern times. Book IV lists specific studies of the period. The detailed Table of Contents substitutes for an index. Annual bibliographies in The Yearbook of Comparative and General Literature (S58) supplement this older work.

S58.   Yearbook of Comparative and General Literature. University of North Carolina [later Bloomington: Indiana University], 1952--.
An annual journal devoted primarily to articles but which includes listings of new translations intended as a supplement to the Bibliography of Comparative Literature (S57). Currently, only works translated into English are listed.

S59.   The Year's Work in Modern Language Studies, 1929/ 30--. London: Modern Humanities Research Association, 1931.
An annual bibliography covering Latin and the romance, Germanic, and Slavonic languages.

S60.   Kearney, E. I., and L. S. Fitzgerald. The Continental Novel: A Checklist of Criticism in English, 1900-1966. Metuchen, N. J.: Scarecrow Press, 1968.
Arranged by nationality (French, Spanish and Portuguese, Italian, German, Scandanavian, Russian and East European); within the nationality entry, alphabetically by author; within the author entry, alphabetically by title. Abbreviations of periodicals cited appear at front.

S61.   Thurston, Jarvis, et al. Short Fiction Criticism: A Checklist of Interpretation Since 1925 of Stories and Novelettes (American, British, Continental) 1800-1958. Denver: Alan Swallow, 1960.
Limited to critical articles in English. Alphabetically arranged by author; within the author entry, alphabetically by title of work. Complete bibliographical entries for books and periodicals analyzed at end.

S62.   Walker, Warren S. Twentieth-Century Short Story Explication: Interpretations, 1900-1966, of Short Fiction Since 1800. 2nd ed. Hamden, Conn.: Shoe String Press, 1967. Supplement I to Second Edition, 1967-1969. Hamden, 1970.
Primarily criticisms in English of well-known short stories by writers of all nationalities. Arranged alphabetically

by author; within the author entry by title.   Index of short
story writers at end.

S63.   Adelman, Irving, and Rita Dworkin. Modern Drama:
             A Checklist of Critical Literature on 20th Century
             Plays. Metuchen, N. J.: Scarecrow Press, 1967.
        English language criticisms of international twentieth-
century plays. Alphabetically arranged by author (no subdivision into nationality; no alphabetical ordering by title of
work). See Preface, p. v for additional bibliographical
sources. Key to Abbreviations follows Preface. Masterlist
of sources cited at end.

Retrospective Bibliographies

S64.   Wing, Donald. Short-Title Catalogue of Books Printed
             in England, Scotland, Ireland, Wales, and British
             America and of English Books Printed in Other
             Countries 1641-1700. 3 vols. New York: Co-
             lumbia University Press, 1945-51. [A revised
             and enlarged second edition of Wing is being pub-
             lished by the Index Committee of the Modern Lan-
             guage Association of America. Vol. I (A-E) ap-
             peared in 1972; the other two volumes are forth-
             coming.
        Wing is a continuation of Pollard and Redgrave's
STC (M24). Entries are numbered. Copies of works listed
are located, though the compiler does not attempt a complete
census. Periodical literature is excluded. Anonymous
works are found under the first word of the title other than
an article. An asterisk denotes a pamphlet under fifty
pages; "bro" denotes a broadside. Many of the works entered in Wing are being microfilmed. Note that Wing includes books printed in the American colonies through
1700.
        Wing is indexed in Paul G. Morrison, Index of Print-
ers, Publishers and Booksellers [in Wing] (Charlottesville,
Va.: University of Virginia Press, 1955). Also see supplement in Huntington Library Quarterly, 16 (1953), 393-436;
J. E. Alden, Wing Addenda & Corrigenda (Charlottesville,
Va.: University of Virginia Press, 1958); and Wing, A Gal-
lery of Ghosts: Books Published Between 1641-1700 Not
Found in the Short-Title Catalogue (New York: Modern Language Association, 1967).

S65.   Sabin, Joseph. Bibliotheca Americana: A Dictionary
             of Books Relating to America, from its Discovery

to the Present Time [1892]. 29 vols. 1868-1936;
rpt. Amsterdam: N. Israel, 1961; rpt. in one
volume--Metuchen, N. J.: Mini-Print Corp.,
1966. [After Sabin's death, the work was completed by Wilberforce Eames (Vols. 14-20) and
R. W. G. Vail (Vols. 21-29).]
Sabin's bibliography differs most importantly from
Evans' (M25) in that Sabin includes not only works published
in the Western hemisphere but also books, periodicals, and
pamphlets about the Americas, wherever these were printed
and in whatever language. Sabin's coverage extends up to
1892; however, since "the Present Time" varied with the
publication date of each volume, coverage is inconsistent.
Arrangement is alphabetical by author, anonymous works being listed under the first word of the title other than an article. Full bibliographical information is given, often including the contents and location of reviews. Rare books are
also located. The most extensive list of Library Location
Symbols is found in Volume 29, 299-305. Despite restric-
tions in scope, discussed in the preface to the last volume,
the Bibliotheca Americana is a monumental undertaking, end-
ing appropriately with the words Laus Deo.

ABSTRACTS, INDEXES, AND DIRECTORIES

Abstracts

*S66. MLA Abstracts of Articles in Scholarly Journals
         [1971--]. New York: Modern Language Associa-
         tion of America, 1973--.
       Three volumes annually, following the arrangement of
the MLA International Bibliography (M7). Volume I contains
abstracts of articles on general, English, American, medieval and neo-Latin, and Celtic literatures, and on folklore.
Volume II is devoted to European, Asian, African, and Latin-
American literatures; Volume III to Linguistics. Articles
are drawn from all relevant scholarly periodicals. Abstracts
(of about two hundred words) are usually prepared by the author of the article. No indexes or cross-references are provided; however, an asterisk after an entry in the MLA International Bibliography indicates that the article has been abstracted. MLA Abstracts contains a Table of Contents and
key to journal abbreviations at the beginning of each volume.

Arrangement is chronological and, within the period, alphabetical by subject (usually literary author's name).

S67.   American Literature Abstracts: A Review of Current
            Scholarship in the Field of American Literature
            [1967--]. San Jose, California [later Los Angel-
            es]: The California State University and Colleges,
            1967--.
Provides summaries, somewhat longer than those in
AES (M26), of periodical articles on American literature published in all relevant journals. Abstracts are written in the
main by the authors of the articles. ALA is arranged chronologically and, within the period, alphabetically by literary author's name. A Book Review Consensus, synthesizing reviews
of recent scholarly books on American literature, follows the
abstract entries. The Finding List of Journals (with abbreviations and addresses) precedes the combined index of literary authors and scholars. ALA appears in June and December.

Indexes

S68.   Social Sciences and Humanities Index [1965--]. New
            York: H. W. Wilson, 1966--. (Formerly Read-
            er's Guide to Periodical Literature Supplement
            [1907-1915], International Index to Periodicals
            [1916-1965].)
Intended, in part, as a continuation of Poole's Index
(S74). Currently an author and subject index to about two
hundred English and American scholarly journals in the humanities and social sciences. (Foreign journals were dropped
in the 1940's.) Author and subject entries are listed in a
single alphabet. Each journal article is entered under its
author and under a number of subject headings. Extensive
subheadings, related headings, and cross-references. Full
bibliographical information. Quarterly with annual cumulations and permanent volumes cumulated for a longer period.
SSHI is more up-to-date than the MLA International Bibliography (M7) or the Annual Bibliography of English Language
and Literature (S44). Indexing such important literary journals as American Literature, Essays in Criticism, Journal
of English and Germanic Philology, and Modern Language
Notes, SSHI is to scholarly periodicals what the well-known
Reader's Guide to Periodical Literature is to popular general
interest magazines.

S69.   British Humanities Index [1962--]. London: The

Library Association, 1963--. (A continuation of
The Subject Guide to Periodicals [1915-61].)
A subject and author index to "all material relating
to the arts and politics," drawn from some four hundred
British periodicals. Subheadings and tables of related headings for broad subjects. Appears quarterly with annual cumulations. The quarterly issues index by subject only; the annual cumulations provide two separate indexes: one by subject, the other by author. Within its field, BHI does for
British periodicals what EGLI (M28) does for American books.
BHI can supplement the MLA International Bibliography (M7)
and the Annual Bibliography of English Language and Literature (S44) for articles from British periodicals.

S70. Index to Little Magazines [1943--]. Denver [later
Chicago]: Swallow Press, 1965--. With retrospective volumes: Index to American Little Magazines [from 1900], comp. Stephen H. Goode (Troy,
New York: Whitson Publishing, 1969-74); and Index
to Little Magazines 1940-1942, comp. Stephen H.
Goode (New York: Johnson Reprint Corp., 1967).
An index of articles and reviews in American little
magazines--avant garde literary journals devoted to aesthetic
reform and experimentation--selected for their high literary
value, degree of permanence, and omission from other indexes. Arranged by author of article and by subject in a
single alphabet. The symbol + indicates the continuation of
the article in subsequent issues. List of Abbreviations and
Magazines Indexed at front of each volume. Further retrospective volumes are projected.

S71. Index to Commonwealth Little Magazines [1964--].
Comp. Stephen H. Goode. New York: Johnson
Reprint Corp. [later Troy, New York: Whitson
Publishing], 1966--.
Goode indexes commonwealth little magazines, using
the same criteria for selection and the same arrangement
found in the American index (S70). Retrospective volumes
are planned.

Biography Index: A Cumulative Index to Biographical
Material in Books and Magazines [1946]. (See
S40.)

S72. Book Review Index. Detroit: Gale Research, 1965--.
Indexes over two hundred periodicals in the fields of
general fiction and non-fiction, humanities, social sciences,

librarianship and bibliography, and juvenile literature. Appears monthly with quarterly cumulations.

S73.   Book Review Digest. New York: H. W. Wilson,
          1905--.
        Summarizes through quotation both favorable and un-
favorable reviews of fiction and non-fiction published in the
U. S. A. About seventy-five popular and general (rather than
specialized scholarly) periodicals are indexed. Length of reviews indicated. Arranged alphabetically by author of book
reviewed. Subject, title, and pseudonym index in each issue.
Appears monthly with semiannual and annual cumulations.

S74.   Poole's Index to Periodical Literature, 1802-81. Rev.
          ed., 1891. Supplements: 1882-1907. 5 vols.
          1887-1908; rpt. Gloucester, Mass.: Peter Smith,
          1958.
        A subject or catchword (important word) index to some
590, 000 articles, fictional works, and book reviews in 479
English and American periodicals. Coverage extends from
1802 to 1907. Creative literary works not lending themselves
to a subject approach are entered under the first word of the
title other than an article. Book reviews of such works are
entered under the name of the author reviewed. Very brief
articles and minor book reviews are omitted. A few British
periodicals are not completely indexed. Bibliographical information lacks inclusive pagination and date. This last can
be found most conveniently in Marian V. Bell and Jean C.
Bacon, Poole's Index Date and Volume Key (Chicago: Association of College and Reference Libraries, 1957). C. Edward Wall, Cumulative Author Index for Poole's ... 1802-
1906 (Ann Arbor: Pierian Press, 1971) is a computerized
index arranged alphabetically by authors of articles cited in
Poole's, noting volume, page, and column of articles and in-
dicating single or multiple references. Poole's has been in
part superseded by the Nineteenth Century Reader's Guide
(S75) and will eventually be wholly superseded by The Wellesley Index (S76).

S75.   Nineteenth Century Reader's Guide to Periodical Lit-
          erature 1890-1899, with Supplementary Indexing
          1900-1922. Ed. Helen Grant Cushing and Adah
          V. Morris. 2 vols. New York: H. W. Wilson,
          1944.
        Indexes fifty-one mainly general and literary periodi-
cals, seven of which are omitted from Poole's (S74). Supplementary indexing for some periodicals extends as far as

1922. Standard subject headings and cross-references. Author, subject, title, and illustrator index to articles, short stories, novels, plays, and poems. Note extensive entries under such broad headings as Drama--Criticisms and Poems. Also indexes book reviews but only under the author of the work reviewed. Many anonymous articles and reviews are identified from publishers' records. List of periodicals indexed at back. For the limited period covered, this is a much more thorough index than Poole's.

S76. The Wellesley Index to Victorian Periodicals 1824-
        1900: Tables of Contents and Identification of
        Contributors With Bibliographies of Their Articles
        and Stories. Ed. Walter E. Houghton. Toronto:
        University of Toronto Press, 1966--. (Two vol-
        umes to date.)
        When completed, The Wellesley Index will provide a
subject, book review, and author index to more Victorian
periodicals than are indexed in Poole's (S74) or in The Nineteenth Century Reader's Guide (S75). Part A of each volume
includes Tables of Contents (excluding poetry) for each issue
of the periodicals covered. Authors are identified with evidence for attribution of authorship. Part B is the author index. Also included is an index of initials and pseudonyms.

        Cumulative Book Index: A World List of Books in the
        English Language. (See S56.)

S77. Index Translationum. Paris: International Institute
        of Intellectual Cooperation [later UNESCO],
        1932--.
        Currently an annual listing of translated books pub-
lished in seventy-five countries. Arranged alphabetically by
French names of countries, then under one of ten broad
category headings found on page 9 of IT, 1970. References
include author, title, translator, place of publication, date
(if other than the year of listing), pagination, special features,
and price. The language in which the original work was
written and its original title are noted in italics. Table of
Contents at front; index of original authors and anonymous
works at back with references to numbered entries. Translations published in countries in which English is either the
primary or one of the primary languages have been cumulated
for the years 1948-68 in Cumulative Index to English Translations 1948-1968, 2 vols. (Boston: G. K. Hall, 1973).

        Thompson, Stith. Motif-Index of Folk Literature.
        (See S13.)

Directories

S78.   Baer, Eleanora A.   Titles in Series: A Handbook for
        Librarians and Students.   2nd ed.   2 vols.   New
        York: Scarecrow Press, 1964.
        _____.   Supplements to the Second Edition.   3
        vols.   Metuchen, N.J.:   Scarecrow Press, 1967-
        74.
        A selective listing of titles published as part of Amer-
ican and foreign series, excluding publishers' series, government publications, yearbooks, and reprints.   Volume I of the
second edition is arranged alphabetically by series.   Within
the series listing, arrangement is numerical according to
publishers' numbers, otherwise chronological or alphabetical.
Numbers at the right hand side of each column are those referred to in the index of authors and titles which constitutes
the first part of Volume II.   The second part of Volume II,
an Index to Series Titles, cites page references.   Each Supplement follows the same format but is complete within itself.   There is no cumulative index to the second edition and
supplements.   A Directory of Publishers appears at the back
of Volume II of the second edition and at the back of each
Supplement.

*S79.   Union List of Serials in Libraries of the United States
         and Canada.   Ed. Edna Brown Titus.   3rd ed.
         5 vols.   New York: H. W. Wilson, 1965.
         The ULS is valuable for locating particular issues of
not readily accessible periodicals in major American and
Canadian libraries.   In this respect, the ULS can be considered a follow-up tool to Ulrich's (M31).   Excluded are
United Nations and many government publications, newspapers,
and ephemora.   (See Introduction to Volume I for complete
listing of exclusions.)   Arrangement is alphabetical by title.
The most recent title--discoverable through cross-references
--contains the main entry.   Information includes title changes,
place of publication, publisher, date of origin, volumes held
by a particular library and that library's lending policies,
and the date publication ceased (indicated by parallel bars).
Abbreviations of cooperating libraries appear at the front of
each volume.   Be sure to study the Explanations (at the front
of each volume) and Sample Entries (only at the front of Volume I) before using the ULS.   Only serials published up to
1950 are included in this third and last edition of ULS.   To
locate periodicals published from 1950 on, see New Serial
Titles 1950-1970 and its quarterly supplements, cumulated
annually.

S80.   Irregular Serials and Annuals: An International Direc-
              tory [1967--]. 2nd ed. New York: R. R. Bow-
              ker, 1971--. Biennial with annual supplements.
       An Ulrich's (M31) for current serials issued annually,
less frequently than once a year, or irregularly. Includes
yearbooks, transactions, proceedings, "advances in" and
"progress in" publications. For those users uncertain of the
periodicity of a particular journal, this directory includes a
title index of all serial publications, giving page references
both to Ulrich's and to Irregular Serials and Annuals. Like
Ulrich's, Irregular Serials is kept up-to-date by Bowker Serials Bibliography Supplement (M31, n. 2).

*S81.   Gerstenberger, Donna, and George Hendrick. Third
              Directory of Periodicals Publishing Articles on
              English and American Literature and Language.
              Chicago: Swallow Press, 1970.
       This directory is an invaluable aid to the creative,
critical, or scholarly writer who wishes to submit his work
to the appropriate periodical. Over five hundred literary and
linguistic periodicals are entered. Information generally includes the name of the editor, address to which manuscripts
should be sent, sponsoring organization, major fields of interest, length of articles, desired style sheet, acceptability
of footnotes, number of copies of manuscript that should be
submitted, payment if any, and copyright arrangements. Arranged alphabetically with subject index at back.

                HISTORIES AND ENCYCLOPEDIAS

                        Literary

*S82.   Watson, George. The Literary Critics: A Study of
              English Descriptive Criticism. 2nd ed. Totowa,
              N. J.: Rowman and Littlefield, 1973.
       An up-to-date history of criticism in England and,
more recently, the United States by the editor of the CBEL
Supplement (M5, n. 2) and of three volumes of the New NCBEL
(M5). Chapter I, First Principles, in which Watson classifies types of criticism and discusses the nature of descriptive criticism, is of value to all students of literature regardless of their particular interests. Ten pages of chapter
bibliographies precede the index. A highly readable work.

S83.   Cunliffe, Marcus. The Literature of the United States.
       3rd ed. Harmondsworth, Middlesex: Penguin,
       1967.
       A concise history through the 1960's including bibliog-
raphy. "Some Dates in American History, " and index. This
work is of particular interest because it offers an English-
man's view of American literature.

S84.   Quinn, Arthur Hobson. The Literature of the Ameri-
       can People: An Historical and Critical Survey.
       New York: Appleton, 1951.
       Contributors: Kenneth B. Murdock, Quinn, Clarence
Gohdes, and George F. Whicher. The Bibliography at the
back of the volume exceeds one hundred pages. A general
bibliography precedes the specific chapter lists. The latter
are arranged in this order: Bibliographies, Works, Letters,
Biographies, and Criticism. Abbreviations used are found
on p. 987. Author-title index at end.

General or Extra-literary

S85.   The Mythology of All Races. Ed. Louis Herbert Gray
       et al. 13 vols. 1916-32; rpt. New York: Cooper
       Square Publishers, 1964.
       Detailed, readable accounts of classical, Teutonic,
Celtic, Slavic, Semitic, Oriental, etc. mythologies in separate
volumes. Each volume has its own Table of Contents; a Bibliography and illustrations will be found at the end of each
volume. Volume XIII is a comprehensive index.

*S86. An Encyclopedia of World History. Ed. William L.
       Langer. 4th ed. rev. and enl. Boston: Houghton
       Mifflin, 1968.
       Useful handbook, chronologically arranged. Maps,
genealogical tables; appendix lists Roman Emperors, Popes,
kings, colleges, etc. Detailed index.

       Steinberg's Dictionary of British History. (See S34.)

       Dictionary of the History of Ideas: Studies of Selected
       Pivotal Ideas. (See S33.)

S87.   International Encyclopedia of the Social Sciences. Ed.
       David L. Sills, 17 vols. [New York]: Macmillan
       and The Free Press, 1968.

Signed scholarly articles on concepts, theories, and
methods of Anthropology, Economics, Geography, History,
Law, Political Science, Psychiatry, Psychology, Sociology,
and Statistics. Biographies and bibliographies. Volume XVII
is the Index.

S88.　The Encyclopedia of Philosophy. Ed. Paul Edwards.
　　　　8 vols. New York: Macmillan and The Free
　　　　Press, 1967.
Signed scholarly articles on eastern and western philosophers, concepts, schools, movements, etc. Bibliographies; index at end of Volume VIII.

S89.　Encyclopaedia of Religion and Ethics. Ed. James
　　　　Hastings. 13 vols. 1908-27; rpt. New York:
　　　　Scribner's, 1961.
An older work but still the best in its field. Authoritative signed monographs on all religions, sects, rites, ethi-
cal movements, moral practices, philosophical ideas and the
individuals associated with them. Also includes related subjects in the social sciences. Bibliographies appended to articles. Alphabetically arranged. Volume XIII contains four
indexes: a general index, an index to foreign words, an index to scripture passages, and an index to authors of articles.

S90.　New Catholic Encyclopedia. 15 vols. New York:
　　　　McGraw-Hill, 1967.
Subtitled "an international work of reference on the
teachings, history, organization, and activities of the Catholic
Church, and on all institutions, religions, philosophies, and
scientific and cultural developments affecting the Catholic
Church from its beginning to the present." Signed scholarly
articles, many of them by non-Catholics, with appended bib-
liographies. Index in Volume XV. Unlike its predecessor
The Catholic Encyclopedia (1907-14), The New Catholic En-
cyclopedia is a religious encyclopedia in the broadest sense.
However, the earlier work is still well worth consulting.

S91.　Encyclopedia Judaica. 16 vols. New York: Mac-
　　　　millan, 1972.
This work supersedes the 1906 Jewish Encyclopedia
but, like its predecessor, covers Jewish history, religion,
literature, and customs from their beginnings to the present.
Social, intellectual, geographic, and biographical information
is included. Signed, scholarly, often exhaustive articles
(the entry on Israel is equal in length to four good-sized

novels), with appended bibliographies. Illustrations. Volume
I is the Index.

S92.   Encyclopedia of World Art.   15 vols.   New York:
            McGraw-Hill, 1959-68.
        Comprehensive (includes architecture, sculpture, etc.).
Scholarly signed monographs.   Extensive bibliographies following major articles.   Excellent plates comprising the second
half of each volume.   Volume XV is the index.

S93.   Grove, George.   Grove's Dictionary of Music and
            Musicians.   5th ed.   9 vols.   New York: St.
        Martin's, 1954.   Supplement [Vol. X], 1961.
        Signed scholarly articles on all aspects of music
(works, theatres, movements, instruments, theory, composers,
performers, musicologists, etc.).   Biographies and bibliographies.   Scants modern composers and popular music.   Supplement contains additions and corrections to earlier articles
and also new articles.

INDEX

Abstracts of English Studies, M26
Adelman, Irving, S63
"A. L. A. " Index to General Literature, The, M28, n. 1
Alden, J. E. , S64
Alspach, Russell K. , M32
Altick, Richard D. , M27, n. 1
American Authors and Books 1640 to the Present Day, S8
American Bibliography (Evans), M25
"American Bibliography" [PMLA], M7, headnote
American Bibliography (Shaw and Shoemaker), M25, n. 2
American Bibliography of Charles Evans, The, M25
American Book Publishing Record, M25, n. 2
American Catalogue of Books, The, M25, n. 2
American Doctoral Dissertations, M27, n. 8
American Heritage Dictionary, The, S28
American Historical Review, M6b, n. 1
American Literary Scholarship, S48
American Literature [periodical], M19a
American Literature Abstracts, S67
American Novel, 1789-1959, The: A Checklist of Twentieth-
    Century Criticism, S51
American Quarterly, M19b
Annals of English Literature, M1, n. 2
"Annotated World Bibliography [of Shakespeare], An, " M19d
Annual Bibliography of English Language and Literature S44
"Annual Bibliography" [PMLA], M7, headnote
Arber, Edward, M24, n. 2
"Articles in American Studies, " M19b
"Articles on American Literature Appearing in Current Pe-
    riodicals, " M19a
Articles on American Literature 1900-1950, S49a
Articles on American Literature 1950-1967, S49b
Articles on Twentieth Century Literature [1954-70], M19i
Ash, Lee, M23, n. 4
Avery, Catherine A. , S24

Bacon, Jean C. , S74
Baer, Eleanora A. , S78
Baird, Donald, S46

Kramer, Elaine Fialka, M35, n. 1
Kramer, Maurice, M35, n. 1
Kuntz, Joseph M., M20
Kurtz, Seymour, M36, n. 2

Laing, John, S1
Landa, Louis A., M19, n. 4
Lang, D. M., M12, headnote
Langer, William L., S86
Lanham, Richard A., M1, n. 4
Las Vergnas, Raymond, M3, n. 1
"LC Catalog," S53
"LC Catalog" Supplements, S54
Leach, Maria, S12
Leary, Lewis, S49a, S49b
Lee, Sir Sidney, M14
Legouis, Emile, M3, n. 1
Lewanski, Richard C., M21
Library of Congress and National Union Catalog Author Lists, 1942-1962, S54
Library of Congress Catalog--Books: Subjects, The, S55
Library of Literary Criticism, A: Modern American Literature, M35, n. 1
Library of Literary Criticism, A: Modern British Criticism, M35, n. 1
Library of Literary Criticism of English and American Authors, The, M35a
Literary Criticism: A Short History, M3, n. 2
Literary Critics, The, S82
Literary History of England, A, M3
Literary History of the United States: Bibliography, M6
Literary History of the United States: History, M4
Literature of the American People, The, S84
Literature of the United States, The, S83
Literatures of the World in English Translation, The: A Bibliography, M21
Little, William, M8, n. 2
Lorenz, Dennis, M23, n. 4
Lowndes, William Thomas, M24, n. 2
Ludwig, Richard M., S10

McNamee, Lawrence F., M27, n. 1
Magill, Frank N., M34, n. 1
Magill's Quotations in Context, M34, n. 1
Malone, Dumas, S37
Manual of Style, A, S32
Masters Abstracts, M27, n. 6